Prince Harming Syndrome

Prince Harming Syndrome

Break Bad Relationship Patterns for Good—
5 Essentials for Finding True Love
(and they're not what you think!)

Karen Salmansohn

DEDICATION

I dedicate this book to my Prince Charming—who's taught me—and keeps teaching me—how to get better and better at loving and being loved. (To quote a favorite poet, Rumi: *"Your task is not to seek for love, but merely to seek and find all the barriers within yourself that you have built against it."*)

Plus, I also dedicate this book to all my Prince Harmings of my past—each of whom have taught me many valuable lessons in love. (To quote a favorite book, "A Course In Miracles": *"What could you not accept if you but knew that everything that happens, all events, past, present and to come are gently planned (. . .) for your own good?"*).

If you're a woman seeking extra support in your search for true love, please write to me at karen@notsalmon.com, friend me at Karen Salmansohn on FACEBOOK, tweet me at notsalmon on TWITTER and sign up for my free BE HAPPY DAMMIT newsletter at www.notsalmon.com

QNY and the QNY colophon are trademarks of the American Map Corporation.

Creative Director and cover illustrations: Karen Salmansohn
Book Design: Seth Labenz and Roy Rub of Topos Graphics

Cataloging-in-Publication Data is available from the Library of Congress

ISBN 978-0843-709261
Printed and bound in Canada
First edition
10 9 8 7 6 5 4 3 2 1

HAPPINESS DEPENDS UPON OURSELVES.

ARISTOTLE

Table of Contents

Introduction/ Confession

Once upon a time I used to suffer from what I call Prince Harming Syndrome—the tendency to date men who were "bad boys"—charismatic, smart, funny, successful, handsome guys who seemed like great catches, until they'd suddenly erupt into a rage over innocuous things (my not making the bed, my being late by 10 minutes, my joking with a male waiter)—or these bad boys would simply prove to be dishonest cheaters.

I remember once I was sharing a dark story about a particular Prince Harming with my buddy Scott, when the man at the next table at the café interrupted.

"Excuse me," this stranger said. "I hope you two don't mind, but I must confess I overheard you talking ... and well ... I'm a psychoanalyst ... and I'm worried about you," he said, staring directly at me. "Do you mind if I give you my free therapy opinion?"

"Not at all," said Scott, answering for me.

"I have nothing to gain by telling you this," the anonymous psychoanalyst began. "I don't want or need your business. But as a psychoanalyst, I cannot help but recognize how this man you're with is emotionally abusive. He sounds like a classic control freak ... with sadistic tendencies ... and you, well, you are a classic masochist . . . since as of right now, you are choosing to stay."

"Masochist?" I repeated.

I looked at Scott. He meekly shrugged.

"But it's good news, too," the anonymous psychoanalyst said. "Masochists always have the most hope for change, because masochists always blame themselves. So . . . search deeply for why you're with this man, your responsibility for having chosen him . . . and get out while you can!" He then grabbed his brown leather briefcase, and whisked out of the café—like some masked psychoanalyst avenger.

I felt both horrified and validated. My Prince Harming had been assessed by a professional to be a sadistic control freak.

And me? I still had yet to figure out why I had chosen him.

In my mind I wasn't a masochist. I'd been tricked. The way advertisers use "bait and switch" my Prince Harming had employed "date and switch." He truly did start out so nice. And he seemed so charismatic, smart, funny, successful.

"You really should end this dysfunctional relationship," Scott urged me. "Trust me. You'll meet and marry a great guy soon enough. You've just got to kiss a lot of frogs before you find your prince."

"I accept that," I told him. "It's just the pigs, dogs and jackasses I mind kissing."

Scott and I laughed heartily at the time. Thankfully shortly after this talk I developed the inner strength and clarity of mind to leave this Prince Harming.

I recognized, however, just because this man was no longer in my life, it didn't mean my masochistic dating tendencies had left too. I needed to do some serious self-exploration, and understand why I had this urge to go towards bad boys—rather than run from them.

Happily I've since broken free from my Prince Harming Syndrome and am living happily ever after with a true Prince Charming—thanks to the empowering insights and techniques I've enthusiastically researched and am now excitedly sharing in this book.

Indeed, it is with extreme empathy and compassionate love that I share the following ideas, philosophies and healthful love strategies!

My Hope: I want to help as many women out there as I can to also break from their curse of being attracted to Prince Harmings—so they, too, can live and love happily ever after.

CHAPTER

Begin Your Love Journey By Writing Your Happily Ever After Ending

When I was a teen, I tried to read the entire Encyclopedia Britannica. My goal: Memorize its contents, be on TV game shows, win lots of cash and prizes, run away from home, move to Manhattan and become a professional writer. I got as far as Asparagus. To this day I still know a little about a lot of words beginning with "A." Some favorites: ants, atoms, astronomy, alchemy, all the Greek gods, goddesses and philosophers—many of whom had names beginning with "A."

Aristotle was a particular childhood crush, because I've always loved philosophy. When I finished reading his one-page encyclopedic write up, I bought books about him. I'd been purposefully saving these dog-eared, underlined Aristotle books, as well as the "A" book of Britannica, all to be used in a novel, where I'd been planning to bless my protagonist with the quirky detail of knowing all things "A."

I recently rediscovered these old Aristotle books when moving apartments. I started flipping through them, and was surprised to discover that Aristotle said a lot of the same things about love and happiness as modern psychologists. Only Aristotle obviously said it first, having been born in the 300s BC. Plus, Aristotle said it truly wisely.

Indeed, much of what Aristotle said hit home big-time—in particular about a sexy, smart, funny, rich, lying, cheating, don't-get-me-started Prince Harming I'd just broken up with. I could almost hear what Aristotle might say to me if we were to chat over souvlaki.

"Mea bene, Karen," Aristotle would say. "You know what your problem was with your ex? He was not your soul mate—but your 'sould' mate—because you sold your soul to be with him. Sure he was sexy, smart, rich, funny—but alas, he was a lying, cheating *asshole*."

"Wow," I'd say. "I can't believe you just said that word!"

"What? *Asshole*?" Aristotle would say with a smile. "Hey, I'm from Greece, so alas I'm no prude."

"Actually, I meant *'soul mate'*!" I'd correct. "You're an intellectual guy—the regaled philosopher who was called The Mind of The Academy by Plato. I'm surprised you believe in something as namby-pamby metaphysical as a *soul mate*!"

"Absolutely!" my fave Greek philosopher buddy Ari would respond emphatically. "Actually, I sort of coined the concept of 'soul mate.' If there'd been a little 'TM' trademark thingie back in the 300s BC, I'd be a very rich man today. I firmly believe caretaking the soul is incredibly important for happiness. I describe a soul mate as a 'soul-nurturing mate'—someone who nurtures your soul—thereby promoting insight and growth. I pushed folks to find soul mates—because in my opinion, real happiness only comes when you stimulate your soul—your core self—and grow into your highest potential. Basically the soul is the ultimate g-spot for happiness."

Of course I'm paraphrasing for my philosopher buddy. But if Aristotle were here, I know he'd agree with my verbal modernization of his timeless truths. Plus, Ari would go on to describe how he views the world as offering . . .

3 Kinds of Relationships . . . Only 1 Brings True Happiness:

I. Firstly, there are **RELATIONSHIPS OF PLEASURE.** These are partners who are all about sex, drugs and rock and roll. You might share soul-less passionate sex and soul-less playful banter—but they're all about pleasures of the body or ego. They never soul-nurture you with insight and growth—so never bring you real-deal happiness. Hence, these partners are souldmates (Prince Harmings)—not soul mates (Prince Charmings).

II. Next up, there are **RELATIONSHIPS OF UTILITY**—a partner you spend time with in hopes of garnering greater wealth, status, fame, power, glory, or beauty by being in their presence. These partners also don't nurture your soul—only your ego. Again, these are souldmates (Prince Harmings)—not soul mates (Prince Charmings).

III. Finally there are **RELATIONSHIPS OF SHARED VIRTUE**. These are partners who stimulate you, challenge you, inspire you, root for you to grow into your highest potential—who nurture your soul. A good example is Jack Nicholson's character in *As Good As It Gets* who says: "You make me want to be a better man." When you prioritize seeking a partner who supports your becoming your best self—instead of just crushing on someone's superficial sexy looks, charisma and wealthiness—you wind up with a soul mate/a Prince Charming/ a definite keeper!

With all this in mind, if you want to be happy in love, you must take the time to see past a guy's *"superficial lures"* (hottiness, funniness, smartness, success, status, power, fame, glory, wealthiness)— and look deep inside his *"superinsidehimself"* true core self.

Unfortunately it's very easy to get hypnotized by *"superficial lures."* In particular, those fumes of chemistry can dizzy a gal into making stupid love choices. It's hugely important to remember: Y*o! Hot steamy chemistry eventually fades—and what's always left beneath is a person's true soul.*

Yes, if you want to be happy, you must seek a good-hearted, ethical, loving soul who brings you *great growth*—not simply a hottie who brings you *great grope!*

CONFESSION TIME:

Another superficially alluring quality I've personally been suckered in by is humor. I am Silly Putty in a friggin' funny man's hands. I once had a boyfriend who even teased me that the secret to getting me into bed was to crack five good jokes in a night. He'd count down his jokes as the night progressed. Unfortunately, funniness is a mere decorative quality—sometimes developed to avoid talking about real life issues. Hence why in the past I've witnessed how after a few months of dating a friggin' funny guy, all that fabulous ha-ha-ha laughter often gives way to tears—when the friggin' funny guy's true character—*true soul*—shows up as one that avoids honest communication, warm empathy and the desire for growth. Hence when I try to connect soul to soul—heart to heart—I am greeted by a gigantic, unmovable whoopee cushion wall.

Basically, friggin' funny is only the tiniest tip of a person. Meanwhile, a person's soul is a person's foundation!

FOR THE RECORD:

Aristotle wasn't against finding someone who is friggin' funny—or friggin' sexy, friggin' smart, friggin' rich, friggin' charismatic. Indeed, Aristotle believed all these pleasure-bringing yummy qualities were good for stirring up passion—which we humans need to feel to be our fullest selves! But Aristotle also recognized *superficial lures* and material goods were simply what he called *"means to the ends"* of happiness—not *"the final ends"* of happiness itself. As Aristotle said:

"Men imagine the causes of happiness lie in external goods. That is as if they were to ascribe fine and beautiful lyre playing to the quality of the instrument rather than the skill of the player."

OR AS I LIKE TO SAY:

"It's just as easy to complain about a rich man as it is to complain about a poor man."

Basically, it doesn't matter how rich a guy is if his behavior makes you twitchy and miserable. Personally, I'd rather split a tunafish sandwich with a Prince Charming than a lobster feast with a Prince Harming.

While on the subject of money, I want to point out that Aristotle was no fan of slackers either. Aristotle recognized that being poor or dating poor brought its own share of problems. Aristotle even strongly admitted that the lack of a certain amount of wealth was as much an obstacle to happiness as deprivation of freedom. He gladly accepted that some wealth was even needed to be happy—just as exciting bodily pleasures were also needed. But once again—

wealth and bodily pleasures were simply mere means to the ultimate ends of happiness—these ultimate ends being to nourish your soul, so you can reach your most esteemed level of self.

With all this in mind, it's essential when you first meet a man, that you take the time to sense if he's a sould-mate Prince Harming—or a soul mate Prince Charming.

Unfortunately, often it's hard to tell the difference between a Prince Harming and a Prince Charming right up-front. In the same way some women wear Wonderbras to make their boobs look better up-front, some men exaggerate who they are up-front with the fake boost of Wondercharm—and WonderhowmuchlongericanIcanactlovingtoyouwithoutcracking.

OR AS ARISTOTLE MIGHT WARN:

"Just because a guy looks good on papyrus doesn't mean he will act good in real life."

Coming up ahead I will give you many helpful techniques for shifting your focus away from a man's decorative socialized self, so you can better develop x-ray vision to see deep into his soul. (Hopefully he has at least a modicum of one!)

Also coming up, I will be expanding more on this theory about the importance of seeking a Prince Charming who stimulates your soul. If right now you're not fully grasping and embracing this concept—not to worry—there's plenty of time. For now, let me further explain one of Aristotle's big beliefs about happiness. Ari put forth that most folks foolishly confuse pleasure for happiness—when the two are incredibly different.

The Big Difference Between Pleasure and Happiness:

I. **PLEASURE** is always temporary—and thereby unsatisfying in the long run—because it's all about immediate fleeting gratification of the body and ego.

II. **HAPPINESS** creates long-haul joy, because it increases your soul's self-development—hence the joy lasts as long as you last—because the joy created becomes an integral part of who you are as a unique, thriving individual.

Basically, Aristotle believed that there are two paths you can take in life:

I. The path seeking conscious nourishment of your soul with insights and growth—or what Aristotle called **THE GOOD LIFE**—and what I will refer to as **LIFE PLAN RIGHT.**

II. The path seeking pleasures of the body and ego— or what I will refer to as **LIFE PLAN WRONG.**

Aristotle believed that you can only be truly happy if you head towards **LIFE PLAN RIGHT**. Basically, life works like this:

Your daily habits over time = **YOUR LIFE**

Lots of non-soul-nurturing habits = **LIFE PLAN WRONG**

Lots of soul-nurturing habits = **LIFE PLAN RIGHT**

Of course, you can afford an occasional Backwards Step towards **LIFE PLAN WRONG**. But too many Backwards Steps just move you plain ol' backwards—away from **LIFE PLAN RIGHT**.

With all this in mind, a big secret to happiness is to stop focusing on finding a Mr. Right—and instead focus on finding **LIFE PLAN RIGHT. MEANING?** When a Mr. Potential Right comes along—you must ask yourself if this guy will lead you to **LIFE PLAN RIGHT** or **LIFE PLAN WRONG**. As you get to know the guy, you should look to see if he (1) offers you exciting growth as well as exciting grope; and (2) has developed good character—so he will be a positive influence on your character development. If he scores two out of two, then the guy is someone who can lead you towards **LIFE PLAN RIGHT**—and a happily ever after future.

Aristotle would very much encourage beginning your love journey with this "final ends" in mind—asking yourself if your Mr. Potential Right is someone who will lead you to **LIFE PLAN RIGHT**. Indeed Aristotle was famous for believing that the best way to start any project—including the project called "Your Life"—is to begin with your final purpose in mind— or what Aristotle calls your **"TELEOLOGY."**

"Shall we not, like archers who have a mark to aim at, be more likely to hit upon what is right?" Aristotle asked.

Right now I will take up Aristotle's advice—and clearly state my **TELEOLOGY** for this book: *I want to give you techniques to break bad relationship patterns for good so you can snag a happily ever after future with a Prince Charming.*

Now it's your turn. How do you envision your **TELEOLOGY** of a happily ever after love future? Below, I want you to write down in great detail what healthful, happy love looks like, sounds like, feels like, smells like, tastes like, quacks like.

_____

_____

_____

_____

_____

_____

I want you to reread and visualize what you've written above—for five minutes, three times day. I'm asking you to do this visualization exercise for neurological reasons—not just Aristotlean reasons. According to brain research, when you train your brain to repeatedly think new positive thoughts, you more permanently change your old way of thinking—by naturally sliding your thinking into these new energized "brain grooves."

Marci Shimoff, the best-selling author of *Happy For No Reason*, explains it like this:

"When you change your thinking to support your happiness, your negative neural pathways shrink and your positive neural pathways widen. Eventually, over time, it becomes easier and more automatic for you to think more positively."

I believe a lot of what contributes to the sadness and downwards spiraling in our lives is a sense of hopelessness. We are resentful that circumstances aren't unfolding as we want, which leads us to doubt we will ever get what we want. Unfortunately every time you imagine worst-case scenarios, you refuel your hopelessness by sending a surge of blood flowing into brain regions associated with depression and anger. If you want to feel happier on a daily basis—and create a brain environment that supports clarity and solutions—then you must consciously think positive thoughts, so you can redirect blood flow in a more positive direction.

A proven effective way to get all this fabulous good blood a-flowing is to engage in positive visualizations!

Neuroscientists have forever sung lively praise about the neural benefits of visualization. It's been consistently shown how simply imagining positive circumstances sends blood flowing from your negative brain regions to your positive ones. In fact, when you merely visualize doing an action, you stimulate the same brain regions as you do when performing that action. For example, if you visualize lifting your left leg right now, you will stimulate the brain region that gets activated when you truly lift your left leg.

Because visualization is so mightily powerful, many professional athletes have trained for events by visualizing successful results. For example, many runners imagine running a race within a specifically speedy goal time. Then when they're out on the track, they make this goal time happen in real time.

I want you to apply this same proven science of visualization to breaking your bad relationship patterns—by teaching your brain to refocus on good relationship patterns.

For the next 30 days I want you to quiet your busy brain and meditate on your *"living happily ever after future with a Prince Charming"* for five minutes, three times a day. Do not envision a specific person you know. Leave room to meet someone even better than who you now know. Make sure you do this assignment by writing it into your calendar, or schedule the visualizations around breakfast, lunch and dinner. Nourish your positive brain regions as you nourish your body.

This *"visualization assignment"* is the first of many assignments I will be giving you—as well as the easiest and most important. There's a famous Japanese principle—called **"KAIZEN"**—that celebrates the joy of doing small tasks that over time add up to the joy of experiencing large life changes.

These small "**KAIZEN**" *visualization assignments* will only take up a total of fifteen tiny minutes in your day. But if you do them, you will change your entire life for years to come. Actually, Kaizen assignments remind me of something funny Woody Allen once said.

A FUNNY BUT WISE WOODY ALLEN QUIP:

Woody says he believes there's life on other planets—and they're far ahead of us technologically. Not because they're light-years ahead—but because they're fifteen minutes ahead. If we all just had those extra fifteen minutes we could accomplish so much more!

THE GOOD NEWS:

You do have those extra fifteen minutes—and so there's absolutely zilcho excuses for you not doing these *"living happily ever after with your Prince Charming"* visualizations for five minutes, three times a day—and keep on doing them for the next 30 days!

Psychologists believe to really drill in a neural pathway shift it helps to do a new habit for 30 days in a row. I agree. And so it seems does Aristotle—who said it well when he said:

"We are what we repeatedly do. Excellence, then, is not an act, but a habit. (...) Thus, it is not enough to perform one act of generosity in order to be generous; it is necessary to act constantly according to the dictates of reason."

Ditto on performing visualizations of your happily ever after future. You must make this your new 30 days in a row habit.

I'm a big believer that these visualizations will help you break bad relationship patterns not only for neuroscientific blood flow reasons—but for other psychological, logical and spiritual reasons. For example . . .

I. You will feel more attractive, imagining yourself as attractive and loved. Indeed, I believe one of the reasons why it's often easier to get a man when you have a man is because you're walking around feeling attractive and loved—which is very magnetic. I've noticed this personally—how the sexiest thing a gal can ever wear to meet new men is another man's arm around her shoulder. I used to wish I could take some of these new men I was meeting when with a beau, put them in Tupperware, store them in my freezer, then defrost these men later when necessary. Great news! When you're doing positive happily ever after **LOVE VISUALIZATIONS** regularly, you will be walking around with this same "positive, confident love energy"—so no Tupperware will be needed for you to have an abundance of male attention! You will have more of a sexy bounce in your step, and an appealing twinkle in your eye, because you will be full of hope and excitement! Basically, emotional pain has a harder time existing when a long-term vision for a happier future takes over! (Oh—and I believe this "positive, confident love energy" will attract more men to you for both psychological and spiritual-universal-energy reasons—both of which I will explain more to you in future chapters!)

II. When you're doing positive happily ever after **LOVE VISUALIZATIONS** regularly, you will want to head out to parties and talk to alluring strangers more often, because you will feel more optimistic about these encounters, leading you to your clearly-seen-and-believed-in happily-ever-after future. Logic prevails: The more conversations you start with strangers, the more you increase your chances of finding your Prince Charming. Babe Ruth not only hit the most homeruns during his time, but he also struck out the most times. Babe never let those strikeouts get him down, because he clearly viewed himself as successful at baseball so he kept on swinging. Ditto with you—and the confidence these happily ever after **LOVE VISUALIZATIONS** will bring you to feel like a total babe who will score big-time with a Prince Charming! A favorite book of mine, *The Course In Miracles*, says: "Patience is easy for those who trust." When you're doing positive happily ever after **LOVE VISUALIZATIONS** regularly, you will have more patience, trust and peacefulness within, that the universe will provide you with the healthful, happy love you are seeking!

III. When you're doing positive happily ever after **LOVE VISUALIZATIONS** regularly, you're teaching yourself to remember the important difference between happiness and pleasure—so you don't get suckered in by a pleasurable-at-the-get-go-but long-haul-unsatisfying souldmate Prince Harming. Which reminds me to remind you:

Yo! That famous phrase I keep referring to is "living happily ever after"—not "living pleasurably ever after"!

Unfortunately, far too many women are seeking to live pleasurably ever after with a Prince Harming in a **RELATIONSHIP OF PLEASURE** or a **RELATIONSHIP OF UTILITY**—and hence they are unhappy in love! In fact 99% of the female clients I coach forget to include 5 absolutely essential traits for happy love in the original Prince Charming **LOVE VISUALIZATIONS** they write down at the beginning of my coaching sessions with them. Once these clients add in these 5 overlooked essential traits for happy love, they improve their love success by 100%!

Curious what these 5 traits might be? Meet me in Chapter 2, and I will divulge all!

CHAPTER

2

The Top 5 Essentials To Look For In A Prince Charming

(NO, they're not sexiness, funniness, smartness, yummy biceps and a good 401k plan!)

efore I share with you the "5 essential traits" that most people forget to include in their *"living happily ever after in love with a Prince Charming"* visualizations, I want to share a fascinating article from the *New York Times*—about the psychology of evil. The article highlighted what it called "The Psychopath Checklist"—a helpful list criminal psychiatrists use to test the potential of someone being a hardcore psychopath, capable of committing repeated evil and violent crimes.

GUESS WHICH TRAITS EVIL PSYCHOPATHS SHARE?

Glibness
Extreme charisma
Need to always be doing something
Feelings of high self-worth
Pathological lying
Proneness to boredom
Emotional unavailability

To my amusement, all these adjectives were also very appropriate to describe my now ex-Prince Harming boyfriend, who was an adorably charismatic, fun, active, confident guy—but in the end turned out to be a two-faced cheater.

THE LESSON LEARNED? Aristotle was right! One of the top traits to look for in a partner is an *appealingly strong character.*

Charles Manson, Stalin, Hitler and Mussolini were all very passionate, charismatic, intelligent, successful guys—but that doesn't mean you should have dated them! Instead, you should be prioritizing finding a partner with mature character values—a good *superinsidehim soul,* which embraces kindness, direct/honest communication, 20/20 listening, empathy, loyalty, constant learning/growth, the ability to compromise—and then some! These good character values will not only come in handy on a day-to-day basis—but during those eventual, inevitable times of conflict.

For example, I can sum up in **"3 THREE ACTS"** the breakdowns and breakups of most relationships— going back as far as Aristotle's day.

A LOVE BREAKUP IN THREE ACTS:

ACT 1: You hurt me.

ACT 2: Because you hurt me I now hurt you.

ACT 3: Because you hurt me I now hurt you and so you hurt me again and so I hurt you again—and downwards spiraling we shall go.

MY POINT:

It's easy to act cold, hurtful or stonewalling to someone you feel has said or done something cold, hurtful or stonewalling to you. It takes a person with strong character values to openly, warmly speak up at the speed of life and dare to express their vulnerabilities with the goal of wanting to embrace kindness, direct/honest communication, 20/20 listening, empathy, loyalty, constant learning/growth, the ability to compromise—and then some! Meaning?

YOU CAN STOP DOWNWARD SPIRALING IN YOUR LOVE LIFE IF:

I. You and your partner value operating from a place of strong character—one not wanting to hurt the other—which only comes when you consciously embrace high-integrity values!

II. You and your partner value seeking self-growth—wanting to responsibly gain insights into how you might be contributing to conflicts—which also only comes when you consciously embrace high-integrity character values!

Seeking strong character values in your partner always matters more than a charismatic personality, because character—not personality—will always be the true chooser of how we behave! *Character*—not personality—will always choose how a person behaves/misbehaves at times of disagreement, disappointment, stress, crisis, temptation, sadness, monetary challenges, illness, vulnerability, misunderstandings.

If you and your partner do not value putting in the effort of acting with strong character values during times of disagreement, disappointment, stress, crisis, temptation, sadness, monetary-challenges, illness, vulnerability, misunderstandings—then your relationship will always suffer!

Indeed, John Gottman, the famed psychologist and researcher who runs The Love Lab, even says he can predict how long a couple will last together not by studying how well a couple gets along—but by studying how well a couple *doesn't* get along.

A relationship is only as strong as its weakest link—how a couple handles their challenges.

THE GOOD NEWS:

If you're involved in what Aristotle called a **RELATIONSHIP OF SHARED VIRTUE**—you will both want to deal with conflict by viewing it as *"a* **LABORATORY FOR GROWTH.***"*

Basically, you must accept right here—right now—if you are going to be involved in a *"living happily ever after with a Prince Charming"* love relationship, then this relationship has a duo function.

The 2 Functions Of A Happily Ever After Love Relationship:

I. A happily ever after love relationship will be a **"DEN OF PLEASURE"**—for fun, companionship, sex, laughter, etc.—which you as a human need—so you can keep your soul alive with passion!

II. A happily ever after love relationship will be a **"LABORATORY FOR GROWTH"**—the ultimate place of challenge for your soul to be nurtured to grow—which you as a human need—so you can keep your soul alive with growth!

Unfortunately, most people only view a relationship solely as a place to experience pleasure—leaving out the soul-ly aspects of love—where you soul-nurture each other to grow!

Indeed, when I ask women to describe what they are looking for in a partner they always list sexiness, funniness, smartness, wealthiness! But these are all personality traits and pleasures of the body and ego—not character values.

IF YOU WANT TO LIVE HAPPILY EVER AFTER IN LOVE YOU MUST:

I. Find a man who values growing as a person!
II. Find a man who truly understands a love

relationship serves the double function of **"DEN OF PLEASURE"** *and* **"LABORATORY FOR GROWTH"**!

If your partner doesn't value growing as an individual, then he won't be ready to deal with non-fun, inevitable conflicts in a high-integrity way. As a result, when non-fun, inevitable conflicts occur, your relationship will suffer—or worse, the guy will run for the hills—end of story, end of relationship!

You know what's funny? How we all know that embracing strong character values really does matter in life and love. Yet, our world mostly offers relationship tips like:

> "Buy these sexy clothes!"
> "Be more successful!"
> "Tighten your buns!"

Nobody ever comes out and says:

> "Yo! Value good strong character values in yourself and others!"

Isn't that weird? I suppose that's because it takes more time, effort and patience to work on strengthening one's character values—and to truly understand another person's inner character—than it does to quickly buy a superficial new sexy outfit, or share a leisurely romantic candlelit dinner.

When you begin to prioritize getting to know a guy's inner character up-front—before you jump in—then it means you're prioritizing protecting your happiness and heart. After all, a guy's character will always be the determinant behind his choosing to behave naughty or nice—thereby making you feel sad or happy.

Think about all those fabulous Prince Charmings in fairy tales! What makes a Prince Charming truly "Princely"? Prince Charmings are made of good strong character fiber! Prince Charmings are noble, kind, and generous with good deeds! Plus, Prince Charmings support a Princess in becoming liberated—so she can venture forth to become her fullest royal potential.

Meanwhile, evil Prince Harmings are just as good-looking, rich, and charismatic as Prince Charmings! A Prince Harming's huge difference is the one spotted within his spotty character! Prince Harmings suffer from major character defects—which then create scenarios which torture and imprison a Princess—preventing her from blossoming into her highest, happiest royal potential!

Meaning? Although you might feel as if you're experiencing "love at first sight" with a Prince Harming, what you're really experiencing is "infatuation at first sight"—because all you're falling for is this man's superficial self, not his *superinsidehim* self.

Coming up I will explain more about the deep differences between "infatuation" and "true love." But for now, let me ask you this . . .

A VERY IMPORTANT QUESTION:

Do you really prefer to place a higher value on a guy's superficial aspects (his sexiness, funniness, smartness, wealthiness)—more than you value his superinsidehim self (his character, his soul)?

If so, then there is a big danger you will wind up involved with a guy who's rude, angry, dishonest, disloyal, hurtful, selfish! As a result, all of his inner bad qualities will make you feel unhappy, insecure, unsafe, just plain frazzled!

REMINDER TIME:

The number one reason to spend time with a guy is that he makes you feel happier—and he is improving your life—not making you more unhappy, insecure, unsafe, just plain frazzled! Another way to explain all this is to make the following confession . . .

CONFESSION TIME:

I used to look at a cute, funny, charismatic guy and think: *"Yum, Yum! I want him!"* Now I know better. Now I look at loving, happy couples—watch the happy, healthy dynamic between the guy and girl—and think: *"Yum, Yum! I want that!"*

MY LESSON/YOUR LESSON:

True love is a **THAT**—not a **HIM**.

Basically, what you should always be seeking in "true

love" is to find a guy with wonderful *superinsidehim character values*—which will then make you feel wonderful within your *superinsideyou self.*

So let me re-ask you that very important question:

Do you really prefer to place a higher value on a guy's superficial aspects (his sexiness, funniness, smartness, wealthiness) more than you value your own happiness and self-esteem?

I don't think so! Happily, you can avoid suffering from getting involved with a Prince Harming, by consciously refocusing away from a man's superficial qualities—and instead refocusing on his *superinsidehim* qualities. In particular, here are the top 5 overlooked traits you should now be seeking first and foremost inside a man— before you even look at his sexiness, funniness, smartness, wealthiness!

THE 5 TRAITS TO SEEK IN A
PRINCE CHARMING:

Prince Charming Trait #1: Does he want to be in a committed relationship? (Basically, does he embrace character values that match with your values for a committed happily ever after future? Are there "value deal breakers" when it comes to marriage, monogamy, kids, religion, etc?)

Prince Charming Trait #2: Does he value growing as a person? (Basically, does he embrace character values that show he has an open and growing soul—values wanting to become his highest potential—owning self-responsibility and seeking insights?)

*Prince Charming Trait #3: Does he understand that a relationship serves 2 functions. It's not solely a "**DEN OF PLEASURE**"—it's also a soul's "**LABORATORY FOR GROWTH.**" (Basically, does he embrace character values that show he absolutely wants a "**RELATIONSHIP OF SHARED VIRTUE**"?)*

Prince Charming Trait #4: Does he make you feel "safe" in the relationship to be your fullest potential? (Surprise: The top feeling a relationship should inspire is "safety." Without safety, you will never arrive at feeling love—because you won't allow yourself to be vulnerable enough for true intimacy. If your man embraces high-integrity character values, then you will trust him enough to reveal your truest self!)

Prince Charming Trait #5: Is your man happy? (Surprise: If you want to live happily ever after, your man has to be happy! If he's unhappy all the time, he will view you through non-rosy, dark-lensed life glasses! You need to find a man who embraces character values that help him be emotionally stable, even-tempered, addiction-free and full of high self-esteem.)

Capiche? Not to worry if you don't presently "capiche"—because I will be explaining all this in greater detail in the chapters ahead. In the meantime, be aware that you should never let your emotional boundaries come fully down (or let your clothes come fully off) until you find out if the man you are with is a 5 out of 5 Prince Charming.

I know how tempting it is to want to rush into the horizontal tango with a hottie Prince you've just met! A lot of women even rationalize that the way to a man's heart is through a woman's vageegee. But if love were indeed found in the vageegee, then why aren't little "vageegee icons" found on Valentine's Day cards? And wouldn't we give vageegee-shaped boxes of candy and write love notes signed:

I (VAGEEGEE ICON)YOU!

I'm kidding—but I am serious! If you start sleeping with a man too soon, you will be risking being hypnotized by his horizontal tango dancing abilities—and will not know until you're already emotionally entrenched if the two of you have a true soul-nurturing connection.

Plus, even in this modern world, you also risk the man respecting you less if you give sex away too quickly. It's timeless psychology. The harder you are to win, the bigger your estimated prize value. Many a man does not want to belong to a club that has touched his member too quickly. It's the ol' Dr. Ejaculate/Mr. Hide Syndrome. As soon as the man comes, he'll want to go.

Hence, if you ever wanna hear "I do," you have to start off saying a lot of "I don'ts."

NOTE:

To enhance sexual willpower, don't shave armpits or legs while out on dates with absolutely hunky Prince Crushes!

Again, I'm kidding—but I am serious! You must resist this urge to horizontal tango too quickly—and take the time to find out if your man has all 5 out of 5 of these essential traits—and make sure your man has strong character values along with those strong pectoral muscles.

Oh ... and guess what? You're not in the clear yourself, little missy. Coming up ahead I will remind you that you must be the change you want to date! You too must become conscious of your character values—so you become a Princess Charming Magnet, which will more assuredly attract and connect with that Prince Charming you're looking to live happily ever after with!

CHAPTER

3

If You Want Your Prince To "Pop The Question," Pop These Questions Up-Front

First of all, I want you to know: I recognize the appealing lure of a Prince Harming. Been there, dated him. There's always something terrific you can find about a Prince Harming. He can be sexy, funny, smart, charismatic. Every jerk has their silver lining. Then again, a Prince Charming is also sexy, funny, smart, charismatic—and not a jerk. So isn't it (duh) wiser to hold out for the jerk-free Prince version?

Admittedly, at first glance these two different Princes appear alike. Trying to speedily differentiate the two can be as daunting as those visual games in magazines—where you're shown two almost-identical drawings, then challenged to identify what's different in each. You stare, and think: "Hmmmmm, these two pics appear the same!" Eventually, as you look closer you see: "Ooooooh . . . this overcoat in picture number one has nine buttons! Pic two only has seven buttons! Aha!"

Similarly, if you look really closely at a Prince Harming you start to see: *"Ooooh! Unlike a Prince Charming, this Prince has two faces, not one. Aha!"*

Trust me. You don't want to date a two-faced Prince.
He'll be a royal pain in your heart. Coming up now,
I will explain more about those 5 essential Prince
Charming traits to seek. Plus, I will give you helpful
questions to ask, so you can more quickly assess
how many faces your Prince is sporting. I don't want
you accidentally blinded by the hypnotizing glint
richocheting off a Prince Harming's bling-encrusted
crown—dazzled and dizzied by his sparkling
external superficial qualities.

*Prince Charming Trait #1: Does he want to be in a
committed relationship? (Basically, does he embrace
character values which match with your values for a
committed happily ever after future? Are there "value
deal breakers" when it comes to marriage, monogamy,
kids, religion, etc?)*

As I mentioned earlier, Aristotle suggests you begin
every journey with your "final ends" in mind. This
philosophy also applies to your making sure up-
front that you and your Prince Crush share the same
"final ends" for your love journey—so you don't
waste precious biological tick-tocking time aimed
in different directions. If you're looking for marriage
and kids within a year, you want to make sure your
Prince Crush is in the same Expectations Ballpark.
If you don't want to get married and have kids,
your Prince Crush similarly should share an Open
Relationship/Zippo Offspring Mindset.

Personally, I believe that for love to truly blossom,
it's helpful if both people want a monogamous
commitment. The minute you fully commit to a

relationship, the static from "emotional confusion" and "intimacy resistance" disappears—and you're able to grow much closer and really build a much stronger, more fulfilling bond.

Some men will tell you up-front that they're not ready for marriage. Listen to them.

Some men will tell you by their behavior that they're not ready for marriage. Watch them.

MAJOR CLUE #1 THAT A MAN IS NOT READY FOR MARRIAGE: He's still living the fraternity life— partying till the later hours, preferring the company of groups, instead of alonetime with you.

MAJOR CLUE #2 THAT A MAN IS NOT READY FOR MARRIAGE: He doesn't feel as if his career is in a place of confidence. If he's feeling lost and/or poor, he will tend to have less of an urge to marry, because he will feel insecure about his readiness to take on a wife and kids.

MAJOR CLUE #3 THAT A MAN IS NOT READY FOR MARRIAGE: It's very nice if your Prince Crush lives in a big house with a gorgeous master bedroom — but not if his parents are presently abiding in this aforementioned gorgeous master bedroom—and your Prince Crush is living in the basement. If you are 100% ready to move forward in an adult mature relationship, you need to find a man who is a 100% mature, self-supporting adult!

Be sure to talk about all your "deal breakers" up-front—religion, money goals, city you want to live in—so these things don't become relationship crashers later.

QUESTIONS TO POP:

I. Ask your Prince Crush if he feels he could live a happy life if he never got married. It will be a fun way to suss out his views on marriage—without being frighteningly direct.

II. Ask your Prince Crush if he has happily married friends—or unhappily married friends. Again, this conversation will get him to reveal his views on his pros and cons (and readiness) when it comes to marriage.

III. Ask your Prince Crush if he has friends who are parents—and if they seem happy parenting. Once he's chatting, ask him if he wants kids—and how many—and how soon.

IV. Ask your Prince Crush what he feels a modern parental unit is like. Do the mom and dad both work? Do you agree or disagree with his role of a mom?

V. Ask your Prince Crush what his views on God are—and how strongly he wants his partner and eventual family to embrace religion.

VI. Ask your Prince Crush if there are other cities he imagines living in. Can you also imagine living there?

Prince Charming Trait #2: Does he value growing as a person? (Basically, does he embrace character values that show he has an open and growing soul—wants to become his highest potential—owning self-responsibility and seeking insights?)

There's a lot of hype about the importance of finding out your paramour's astrological sign to better predict your future. I say: Pshaw! You should look for these "positive signs" instead:

Your Prince Crush comments on news stories with a sense of empathy and awareness.

Your Prince Crush asks you lots of questions—and listens to your answers.

Your Prince Crush doesn't just talk in Ego-Monologue.

Your Prince Crush is up for sharing the good times and bad times.

If your Prince Crush is having a problem at the office, he'll openly share it, rather than shelf it.

Basically, all of these positive signs are clues that your Prince Crush has an open and growing soul. And you need a man with an open and growing soul—so you can be open and growing alongside him.

You've heard stories about how somebody in a couple felt as if they were growing—and their partner was not—and so the relationship ended. You don't want that to be you!

Plus you want a partner who embraces operating with empathy, compassion and self-responsibility— so he'll behave lovingly when inevitable conflicts arrive on the scene.

BY THE WAY:

Just because you're looking for a man of good character doesn't mean your Prince Crush needs to be 100% perfect. (You're not seeking a *Saint Charming!)* Personally, I believe finding a man who makes mistakes in life is not necessarily a "bad thing"—as our culture often has us believe. At least if a man is out there blundering, he's out there risking and exploring. More importantly, you need to suss out if your Prince Crush is eager to learn from his mistakes! To err is human. To become a better person because of your erring is divine!

QUESTIONS TO POP:

I. Ask your Prince Crush to describe his friends. Listen to hear if his friends have good character. Remember: The poisoned apple doesn't fall far from the tree!

II. Ask your Prince Crush to fess up to any immoral behavior: Cheating, stealing, lying, binge-drinking, aggression—like punching someone, or being mean to a pet. If he has a scary tale to tell, ask him how much reflection for his bad behavior he's experienced. Listen closely to hear how strongly he desires change.

III. Ask your Prince Crush why his last relationship ended—and what he's learned. If he blames breakups 100% on his partners, this is a bad sign he's not an open and growing soul.

IV. Ask your Prince Crush how he has grown in the last few years. Does he talk about how he'd like to grow in any specific areas?

V. Ask your Prince Crush what his weaknesses are. Listen to hear if he shares how much he wants to strengthen up his trouble spots.

VI. Does your partner need to drink alcohol to talk openly with you? Do you intuit he's hiding anything from you? Be forewarned if his stories feel inconsistent—or are peppered with incongruities.

Prince Charming Trait #3: Does he understand that a relationship serves 2 functions. It's not solely a **"DEN OF PLEASURE"**—it's also a soul's **"LABORATORY FOR GROWTH."** (Basically, does he embrace character values that show he absolutely wants a **RELATIONSHIP OF SHARED VIRTUE?**)

One of the big reasons I love Aristotle is that he loved *"sensory pleasures"*—unlike his predecessor Socrates who said:

"To want nothing is divine; to want little is the nearest possible approach to the divine life."

In regard to desire and pleasure, Aristotle was very different from both Socrates and Plato, who considered food, wine, sex, music, art—all of life's various pleasures—to be dangerous evils. Contrarily, Aristotle accepted that our human nature is meant to enjoy passions. But he also believed our human nature is simultaneously blessed with reason ("consciousness"), which we can use to regulate our passions—keep them within a moderation point—if we so choose. And we must choose—because we must embrace both two out of two of these natural human tendencies—both passion and reason ("consciousness)—if we are to truly live out our perfection as humans—and thereby be truly happy.

Basically, Aristotle very much accepted that it's highly human to be pulsating with lots of sensory needs. Our soul even needs to be stimulated with sensations for it to fully thrive. Sure, we can live without satisfying our sensory pleasures—but according to Aristotle we cannot live well. We cannot live what Aristotle called **THE GOOD LIFE**—and what I've renamed **LIFE PLAN RIGHT**. If you as a human foolishly attempt to live without sensory pleasures, you will only be living a small, shrunken life! After all, when you live without sensory pleasures, you are cutting off circulation to your soul. Basically, numbness is dumbness! You need stimulation of your body and senses to be a truly happy person! For this reason, Aristotle believed it was good to indulge in hot sex, yummy foods, thrilling live concerts, stylish Christina Laboutin shoes (my favorite vice)—with two caveats:

I. You must indulge in sensory pleasures to within a moderation point.

II. You must not make these sensory pleasures your final ends in life! You must understand they're merely means to get you to your final ends —which is always to become your highest potential.

With all this in mind, if you want to be happy in a relationship you must accept that it has to exist to serve two functions: (1) It's a **DEN OF PLEASURE**; (2) It's a **LABORATORY FOR GROWTH**. Below are two sets of questions to suss out who your Prince Crush is deep inside when it comes to both these functions.

QUESTIONS TO POP
(DEN OF PLEASURE):

I. Lust and love are as different as night and day. If your Prince Crush only wants to see you at wee hours of the night, it's only lust. If he wants to spend the more precious daylight hours on weekends with you, you're heading towards real-deal love, baby!

II. Does sex leave you breathless—or breath-full? You need to have a good sex life to be happy—and to help you through those bumpy times. Yes, there's nothing like some good humpy to help you through the bumpy! Do you have agreed-upon expectations for each of your sexual giving and receiving practices? Do you have agreed-upon expectations for each of your affection-giving and affection-receiving practices? Have you had "the talk" about total sexual exclusivity and clearly agreed to it?

III. The hell with a hot sex life. Do you have a hot laughter life? Laughter will get you through hard times—especially when hard times are hardless times. As Aristotle said: "Laughter is a bodily exercise precious to health."

IV. Do you and your partner enjoy doing activities having nada to do with moola? Picnics in the park? Cooking at home and watching old movies? Putting cheese-whiz on a Ritz—not putting on the Ritz! How many different kinds of sports and hobbies do you and your partner like to do together? Do you and your partner have open and compatible expectations on vacations and free time?

V. Have you talked directly with your Prince Crush about your money values? Do you both know how much you both need to be happy—and why? Do you share the same monetary priorities? How do you each prioritize spending? Trips. Clothes. A fabulous home. Charity events. College Education. Plastic surgery. Saving rainforests. Are you both compatible when it comes to being high vs. low spenders?

VI. Good looks fade. But a bad personality is forever. Does your partner titillate your mind as much as your body? Do you respect your partner's beliefs and knowledge and insights—and vice versa? Lust, love and like. Your ideal partner should feel all 3 out of 3 for you—and vice versa. A good royal coupling is a "passionate best friendship."

QUESTIONS TO POP
(LABORATORY FOR GROWTH) :

I. Keep an eye out not only for how much your Prince Crush loves you—but for how good your Prince Crush is at loving. Does he express feelings of love for friends and family? Does your Prince Crush have a lot of lasting, healthy friendships—or hardly any? Does your Prince Crush always tell stories about bad dynamics— fights and skirmishes? Or does he seem to get along easily, even swimmingly, with others?

II. People have different capacities for intimacy and togetherness. Problems arise when there's an ability mismatch. Ask your Prince Crush what he feels best helps to create true intimacy and love.

III. Does your Prince Crush truly value open, honest communication? When you're upset or need nurturing, does he deal with your problems at the speed of life—or shut down or attack? Ask your Prince Crush what he thinks about the concept that "relationship challenges are opportunistic vehicles to help you learn how to get better at receiving and giving love."

IV. Does your Prince Crush choose to express his full range of feelings? Does he seem emotionally generous—or emotionally stingy?

V. What's one of the sexiest qualities to look for in a partner? The ability to listen and compromise! Why? Because listening/compromising keeps you feeling appreciated/connected. If you've had a disagreement— even over something small like which movie to see or what place to eat—have you experienced your Prince Crush being able to listen and compromise? Have you heard him utter the four sexiest words ever: "I'm sorry. You're right!"

VI. Has your Prince Crush talked with you about lessons he's learned about pain and disappointment? Does he show signs of empathy for your pain and disappointment? Does he do behaviors of nurturing and supporting?

Prince Charming Trait #4: Does he make you feel "safe" in the relationship to be your fullest potential? (Surprise: The top feeling a relationship should inspire is "safety." Without safety, you will never arrive at feeling love—because you won't allow yourself to be vulnerable enough for true intimacy. If your man embraces high-integrity character values, then you will trust him enough to reveal your truest self!)

Before you get on the road to "forever after," you want to make sure you love who you are being when you're with your Prince Crush. After all, you'll be spending the rest of your life with you as well as your prince—so you better damn well love the you who you will be!

Unfortunately, sometimes we gals pick guys who look great on paper (funny, sexy, smart, charismatic) but don't act so great in real life. These Prince Harmings wind up being condescending, inconsistent, bad-tempered, judgmental, insensitive, rude, etc. Quite simply, they don't create an environment where a gal can feel safe to speak up and be her truest self.

For this reason, you need to prioritize feeling "safe" in your relationship, because true happiness can only come when you're able to be your truest self—growing into your best-est self.

Jim Collins in his terrific book, *Good To Great*, explains in great detail how one of the most important qualities necessary to grow a company from good to great is the ability to speak "harsh truth"—be a front-stabber, as I like to say. (Inspired by a famous saying: *"A friend is someone who stabs you in the front.")*

Collins explains how harsh-truth-speaking is the only way a company can gain needed blind-spot insights—so the company knows what's holding it back from greatness. Because harsh-truth-speaking is so essential to growth, companies that are run by nice, empathic bosses tend to be the ones which grow from "good to great"—because employees are less afraid to harsh-truth-speak to nice, empathic bosses. This applies ditto with a Prince Charming. It's far easier to truth-speak with a nice empathic Prince Charming than a tyrant Prince Harming.

Basically, the more you feel safe to be truthful with both bosses and boyfriends alike, the more you'll strengthen bonds—and grow from a good bond to a great bond.

For this reason, you must really focus on how your Prince Crush makes you feel within your *superinsideyou self*. Does he make you truly feel happy, confident, inspired, peaceful, open to communicating, free to be your fullest you? Or does he make you feel insecure, unsafe, frazzled, neurotic, totally crazy? The funny comedian Woody Allen once wrote:

"To love is to suffer. To avoid suffering, one must not love. But then, one suffers from not loving. Therefore, to love is to suffer; not to love is to suffer; to suffer is to suffer. To be happy is to love. To be happy, then, is to suffer, but suffering makes one unhappy. Therefore, to be happy, one must love or love to suffer or suffer from too much happiness."

Okay. I admit it. I find this Woody quote funny as hell. But I am here to remind you: Your love life should not be your suffering life! (Oh . . . and Woody Allen's also wrong about his cooking methods. Woody instructs: *"Who bothers to cook TV dinners? I suck them frozen.")*

It's essential you find a man who makes you feel safe to drop your guards—along with your panties. Your partner should always create an environment where you feel safe to come out from behind your fancy-shmancy socialized self exterior, and be your most authentic self! Yo! It's called "finding a soul mate" for a reason! Being with a "soul mate" is about connecting soul to soul. If your soul is not coming out to play, you will never feel connected—and thereby never feel like you've found your soul mate. End of story—and so it will be a story without that yearned for happily ever after end!

QUESTIONS TO POP:

I. A lot of women say the best way to catch a man is to play games. Not me. (Unless it's naked Twister— then I'm all over it.) I believe if you use game-playing as bait, you lure in a game-playing guy. However, if you use "truth and open communication" bait, you reel in the guy who eats that good stuff up. Does your partner inspire you to be the most open and communicative non-game-player you can be? If you had a bad day at the office, would you share it—or shelf it? Do you need to drink alcohol to talk openly with your partner?

II. Does your partner have 20/20 listening skills? Does he talk in monologue or ask you questions about you—and pay attention to your answers?

III. Does your Prince Crush value being communicative, verbally appreciative, openly caring —because they know the gains of true intimacy far outweigh the pains?

IV. Size does matter. You must look for a partner with a really big heart. Have you seen evidence that your Prince Crush is intrinsically warm, open, kind—or the opposite? Have you witnessed your Prince Crush doing small acts of kindness (leaving a very big tip, helping someone with his or her shopping bags)? Does your Prince Crush donate time, money and energy to good causes or charities?

V. Are you and your Prince Crush able to talk about the status of your relationship openly—or does he leave you guessing how he feels? Have you ever felt the need to snoop in his e-mail box or text messages? Have either of you ever cheated? Was this fully resolved? Do you each feel fully confident in your commitment to each other?

VI. Ask you Prince Crush if he feels partners should be honest about everything—and if not, what shouldn't they be honest about? Remember: It's relaxing to love someone you trust—someone you know will not hide parts of their life—and will happily offer up the truth, without you feeling as if you are yanking it out of him.

Prince Charming Trait #5: Is your man happy? (Surprise: If you want to live happily ever after, your man has to be happy! If he's unhappy all the time, he will view you through non-rosy, dark-lensed life glasses! You need to find a man who embraces character values that help him be emotionally stable, even-tempered, addiction-free and full of high self-esteem.)

Want a happy, healthy relationship? It's far easier to find it with a happy, healthy Prince Crush. If your Prince Crush is consistently unhappy, it's as if he is giving off "a smell of unhappiness"—which can create two problems:

I. Firstly, your Prince Crush is often not aware that this "smell of unhappiness" is emanating from him. He just knows "unhappiness is abounding." The risk? Your Prince Crush will sniff around, see you close by, then blame that unhappy stench all on you!

II. Secondly, your Prince Crush's bad unhappiness smell can ruin your mood and weigh you down. Sure, it's good to be there to support your partner—but not if you're doing it so much it makes you potentially depressed too. Psychologists and biologists even have a name for this: "emotional contagion." They claim unhappiness spreads not just because of obvious psychological reasons—but primal, evolutionary ones. *"The original form is the contagion of fear and alarm,"* said Frans de Waal, a psychologist and primate expert at Atlanta's Emory University. *"You're in a flock of birds. One bird suddenly takes off. You have no time to wait and see what's going on. You take off, too. Otherwise, you're lunch."*

TRANSLATION: Getting caught up in another's negativity is a hardwired survival mechanism.

Psychologists believe that "contagion theory" is also a form of hardwired human mimicry—our instinctive human tendency to unconsciously imitate facial expressions, vocalizations, postures and body movements. For example: If someone scratches their nose, you might suddenly feel your nostrils twitch. Or if someone yawns and stretches and gets sleepy, you might yawn and feel more tired, too. Mimicry is such a strong foundation of our human emotional development that even at a mere 1-hour old, a newborn infant will be hardwired to mimic a person's facial gestures. Hence why you can smile at a 1-hour old baby, and this 1-hour old baby will smile back!

TRANSLATION: Our built-in human system for mimicry explains why we humans can transfer our good and bad moods to each other—if we aren't careful!

Numerous studies have shown how when one person in a romantic coupling gets depressed, the other becomes more depressed. Psychologists believe this transfer of emotions is yet another form of empathy. In London's University College, psychologist Tonia Singer and colleagues used brain scans to explore empathy in 19 romantic couples. She hooked both individuals to brain scans. One partner in the couple was given a slight electric shock while the other partner watched. Each of their scans showed identical brain reactions. Although only one partner was shocked, both partners' pain centers lit up—as if both had been jolted.

On a more happy note . . . Howard Friedman, a psychologist at University of California at Irvine thinks "emotional contagion" is also why some people can inspire others to positive action—like a a joyous/exuberant partner in a romantic coupling. Friedman believes it's because the happy person's happy facial expression, happy voice, happy gestures and happy body movements conspire to transmit happy emotions.

QUESTIONS TO POP:

I. Do you know the dirtiest of details about your partner's truest mental health history? Is he bipolar? On medication? Has he ever had a meltdown?

Does he have anger management issues? Drug or alcohol addictions? Ask your man directly to explain why and how he broke up with his last relationship. Listen for long-term anger and Drama King stories.

II. One of the top big determinators of happiness is high self-esteem. It's corny but true—it's hard for someone to love you happily if they're not happy with themselves first. Do you sense your Prince Crush feels proud of who he is in his life? Does he allow people to walk all over him? Does he treat himself with self-nurturing and self-respect?

III. Does your Prince Crush eat nutritionally, exercise, get enough sleep? Does he drink in excess?

IV. Another big determinator of happiness is having a Grand Quest—a passion. Does your Prince Crush have a job or hobbies that bring him tremendous joy?

V. Yet another big determinator for happiness is the person having a **BALANCED WHEEL OF FORTUNE**—*so they can roll along smoothly in life. Does your Prince Crush receive joy not only from your relationship, but from each of these areas: career, friendship, spiritual awareness, fitness, entertaining fun activities, family, community involvement.*

VI. *Fess up. Are you truly happier with your partner in your life?*

So, that's the last question for you to ask and ponder. I really encourage you to take the time to ask and ponder all these questions—before you jump into bed with a man. I promise that it's truly worth your time and effort to consciously shift focus away from seeing your partner's fabulous *superficial self*—so you can suss out if your partner has a fabulous *superinsidehim* self. I know a lot of gals don't want to put in this time and effort—because they say they're being "romantic," and just want to go for it.

LISTEN UP:

Claiming you're jumping in quickly because you're being *"romantic"* is just a euphemism for saying you're *"impatient, lazy and shallow."* Oh—and *foolish* too! After all, if you don't put in the time and effort to pop these questions, you could be due for painful misbehavior side affects. Aristotle said it well when he said:

"Wishing to be in love is quick work, but love is a slow, ripening fruit."

I recognize that in today's speeded-up, channel-surfing, Red Bull-slugging, now-NOW-NOW world, we can often find ourselves desiring immediate gratification. But that's as foolish as biting into a green banana! You must let love ripen!

Now that you've asked and pondered, I want you to scribble. Take some time now to rewrite your *happily ever after with a Prince Charming* visualization—adding in the 5 essential traits you now know you must absolutely seek in your Prince Charming. Include in your visualization that in this relationship you feel "safe." When you perform this visualization, center in on this feeling of "calm safety" with your partner. Go ahead. Write it all down now in stream of consciousness words, while these new thoughts are still top of mind. Remember not to write your man's specific name into the visualization. You must leave room for someone you have not yet met to enter into your life—as there might be someone even more right for you than the man you're presently crushing on. Plus, your present Prince Crush might turn out to be a Prince Harming, and you don't want to become too emotionally invested in the wrong man too quickly. For a suggestion of a good visualization to base yours on, read mine on page 218.

_____

_____

_____

_____

_____

_____

_____

_____

_____

_____

_____

_____

_____

_____

_____

_____

_____

_____

_____

_____

_____

_____

_____

_____

_____

_____

_____

_____

_____

_____

Coming up in the next chapter, I will give you some helpful insider information on how to resist the lure of a Prince Harming—so you can experience what Aristotle called **"EDUCATION OF THE SOUL."**

CHAPTER

4

Break The Prince Harming Curse Of Your Past

You know that expression, the more things change, the more they remain the same? Aristotle said it first. Sort of. Aristotle wrote about how all the universe is in constant motion, always changing. However, there is one specific thing that remains forever the same: your internal seed of potential, or what he called your "**ENTELECHY**." Aristotle explained how everything on this planet possesses within itself its own "**ENTELECHY**"—its unique seed for potential growth.

FOR EXAMPLE:

Consider an oak tree! Its journey to oakdom all begins with a teeny seed. Of course, certain changes and stages have to happen on this seed's route to development. But its potential is constant: to become an oak tree. The seed is never meant to become a petunia plant, an umbrella, a pizza.

FOR ANOTHER EXAMPLE:

Consider You! Every seven years, every cell in your human body will change completely, be gone, poof. Yet in seven years, You will miraculously always wake up as You . . . at least some form of You. How is this possible?

ARISTOTLE'S METAPHYSICAL EXPLANATION

Inside You is forever your original You Seed, guaranteed to be growing You into a You Of Some Variety. Just as an oak seed can grow itself into a Mighty Oak or a Stunted Bonsai Oak, your environment and experiences can shape You—or misshape You. You can grow You into a Mighty Human Being or stunt You into a Bonsai Being.

According to Aristotle, there is always a reason for everything that happens. Every experience is meant to shape you, define you—and hopefully, alas, grow you into the **MIGHTIEST YOU** possible.

Interestingly, it's a known fact that trees that endure the stormiest wind conditions grow the strongest trunks and branches. In contrast, trees that grow in nonwindy environs tend to be more fragile, twiggy, weak.

TO KEEP THIS TREE ANALOGY GOING

*You can choose to grow into your **MIGHTIEST SELF**, if you choose to consciously tap into a fabulous unique human perk that Aristotle called "nous poetikos"— which roughly translates into **CONSCIOUS INSIGHT**. When you tap into **CONSCIOUS INSIGHT**, you will find that you more easily bend with stormy winds— instead of angrily resisting them, and getting blown sideways.*

IN OTHER WORDS:

You know that nasty breakup you endured? You can choose to lovingly rename the experience: "The breakup that led to the breakdown that led to the breakthrough!"

IN MORE OTHER WORDS:

*You can experience an empowering Growth Opportunity Breakthrough—via tapping into that fabulous unique human perk known as **CONSCIOUS INSIGHT.***

GREAT NEWS:

*You are guaranteed a happier life if you consistently choose to tap into **CONSCIOUS INSIGHT**—and consciously keep your "life end goal" in mind—to become your **MIGHTIEST HUMAN BEING SELF.***

Of course when things are going badly, there's always a tempting urge to Bonsai Yourself—to shut down and shut off—to give in and give up—to get bitter, resentful, angry, spiteful, depressed, self-destructive, antisocial—and all before breakfast!

This soul-shutting-down tendency reminds me of a horror movie I once saw, where unconscious, soul-less Zombies were walking around miserably taking bites out of happy, alive, soulful people—then these new folks newly bitten suddenly joined the throng of unconscious, soul-less biting Zombies!

*MEANING? If you've had a bad experience being bitten by an unconscious, soul-less Zombie, you must choose to put in the **CONSCIOUS INSIGHT** of resisting the urge of joining the throng of unconscious, soul-less biting Zombies—and choose to stay a good, loving, soulful person aimed at becoming your **MIGHTIEST HUMAN BEING SELF.***

FACT: Bad things—and bad people—happen to everyone on this planet.

FACT: You cannot control much of what happens in life. Your life is a lively fusion of free will merged with destiny.

*FACT: Thanks to the perks of free will, it's up to you to choose to tap into **CONSCIOUS INSIGHT** and become your **MIGHTIEST HUMAN BEING SELF**. It's up to you to morph all of your pain into all of your gain. It's up to you to view all of your tormentors as your mentors—teaching you valuable lessons that help you to grow into your highest self.*

*FACT: **CONSCIOUS INSIGHT** is the most powerful growth formula available to sprinkle on your potential seed for growth—your **ENTELECHY**—your soul—so you can grow into your **MIGHTIEST HUMAN BEING SELF.***

Aristotle even went so far as to say that he believed **CONSCIOUS INSIGHT** is the highest form of knowledge—more so than factual book knowledge—because it is the only knowledge that helps you grow into your **MIGHTIEST HUMAN**

BEING SELF—and growth is always a human's number one happiness determinator.

Shocking, huh—how Aristotle—a hungry lover of reading—preferred the knowledge of personal experience and its accompanying insights—over any knowledge simply gleaned from a book. Basically, Aristotle believed when it comes to substantial self-evolution, books and lectures will only inch you forward so far. You really have to experience **"A THING"** to understand **"A THING."** On this point, Aristotle differed very much from his teacher Plato, because Aristotle was a philosopher who proselytized the strong-as-espresso belief that experience is 1000% necessary for full understanding of **"A THING."**

For this reason, Aristotle believed even bad experiences had the potential to be good for you—as long as you used them to teach yourself **"A THING"** or two—via **CONSCIOUS INSIGHT**!

Aristotle believed **CONSCIOUS INSIGHT** has many fab perks: You can tap into it to seek helpful and happy interpretations for whatever happens in your life. You can use it to look for meaning, purpose, shared connection with other humans . . . to appreciate art, music, wine, discovery of all kinds— all of which aids and abets you into developing into your **MIGHTIEST HUMAN BEING SELF.**

Admittedly, **CONSCIOUS INSIGHT** also comes with one big disadvantage: It can hurt like hell.

AS ARISTOTLE ADMITTED:

"To perceive is to suffer."

For this reason I have personally renamed **CONSCIOUS INSIGHT** with the more honest nickname of **PAIN-A-RAMIC VISION**—because **CONSCIOUS INSIGHT** is always accompanied by temporary pain—which eventually happily gives way to wider perspectives on **"A THING"**—or two.

Granted, it's tempting to want to avoid the temporary pain of **PAIN-A-RAMIC VISION.** Unfortunately, it's essential you put up with its fleeting sting—otherwise you will be forced to endure even greater pain in your life—the pain of repeated patterns of disappointment and failure. Carl Jung said it well when he said:

"The foundation of all mental illness is the avoidance of legitimate suffering."

How true. You must never confuse "repression of your pain" for "inner peacefulness." If you choose to completely ignore your pain, you will risk winding up expressing it pathologically—by reliving patterns of failure, acting out passive-aggressively, becoming perpetually cynical, or taking on an addiction.

Freud called this urge for duplicating your past in your present **"REPETITION COMPULSION"**—and explained how you as a human have two methods for keeping your past alive:

I. Your repeated pattern of the same negative thoughts.

II. Your repeated pattern of the same negative actions.

Meaning, you can try to relive your past by:

I. Overdoing your daily negative thoughts about your past—both on a conscious and a subconscious level.

II. Choosing current situations that are doppelgangers to your past—being led to these familiar reenactments through the hypnotic trance of your subconscious.

SIMPLY PUT:

You are the common denominator in all your relationship problems! If you keep finding yourself saying *"All the men I date are friggin' nuts!"*—you must ask why you keep picking men who are friggin' nuts—because there are loving/sane men out there! In fact, wherever there's an all encompassing *always*, *all* or *never* in your life, it's a sign that your mischievous subconscious is setting you up for failure by consistently leading you back towards these repeat performances!

In many ways, for many reasons, the subconscious should actually receive bigger and better billing than mere "sub" status. It should be called the "over-and-above-conscious"—because it makes so many of your life decisions. Your subconscious is in charge of how many sick days you get—how messy your home is—and definitely how messy your love life is. Your subconscious is also why your diary can often read like Mad Libs. For instance . . .

Dear Diary,

I'm _____ (mad, resentful, depressed)
that _____(my past paramour, present
paramour, future paramour) doesn't _____(listen
to me, respect me, love me more). It reminds me
of what happened _____ (last week, last
month, last year, next week, next month, next year)
with _____ (my past paramour, present
paramour, future paramour).

Basically if you're not leading your happiest love life, it's because your subconscious has created an incomplete, shortsighted map of the world—and through **REPETITION COMPULSION** is leading you back to the same old situations and people! If you're a "foodie," a good analogy to describe **REPETITION COMPULSION** is to say it's as if your subconscious has given you a very limited menu of life options—and so you keep repeatedly ordering the same lousy nauseating food options—which is really dumb—because in reality, you have many more yummy food ordering selections available!

It's funny how we humans love to blame other people and bad luck for our failures and challenges. The truth: More often than not our repeated patterns of disappointment are due to our own damn self—and our own damn subconscious! Much of what your present subconscious foolishly believes was learned in your childhood. Basically, it's as if we all have a **PORTABLE CHILDHOOD** we take with us as we head into adulthood—and we try to find new people to reportray old family members. So if you had a mom who was very Mommy Dearest—and shrieked at you all the time—you will attempt to recreate "Shriek Two, The Saga Continues"—by dating a Prince Harming.

Another way to describe **REPETITION COMPULSION** is to explain it as a system that keeps you stuck in **MASOCHISTIC EQUILIBRIUM.** Basically, if you grew up in a home where you were taught love is 60% happiness, 40% pain—then later as an adult you manage to create a love life full of 97% happiness, only 3% pain—you will start to feel twitchy. Your subconscious will then step in and self-sabotage— bringing your happiness level back down, down, down to your familiar comfort zone—or rather familiar discomfort zone—your **MASOCHISTIC EQUILIBRIUM.**

A MAJOR CLUE YOU'RE SUSPECT FOR MASOCHISTIC EQUILIBRIUM: You are known amongst your friends for loving to "enterpain" them with amusing "love stories," full of woes, conflict, miffed-ness.

Modern happiness researcher Martin Seligman calls this tendency for repeating painful scenarios **LEARNED HELPLESSNESS**. Seligman advises that the best way to snap out of your **LEARNED HELPLESSNESS** trance is to teach yourself to let go of your Negative Explanatory Story about your life's past pain—and start retelling a Positive

Explanatory Story. Basically, if you want to change the negative patterns of your love life, you gotta teach your old brain some new tricks—train your brain to tap into that big-time force of **CONSCIOUS INSIGHT**—and thereby put up with the temporary pain of **PAIN-A-RAMIC VISION**. For this reason, back in the 300s Aristotle said:

*"**COURAGE** is the first of human qualities because it is the quality which guarantees the others. (. . .) You will never do anything in this world without **COURAGE**. It is the greatest quality of the mind next to honor."*

So, just as growing into your **MIGHTIEST HUMAN BEING SELF** is your number one purpose in life, tapping into **COURAGE** is your number one virtue needed to get you there! It takes **COURAGE** to be fully honest with yourself about the pain in your past. It takes **COURAGE** to recognize you might have been foolishly repeatedly mis-aiming yourself towards **LIFE PLAN WRONG**, because of your subconscious' limited beliefs. It takes **COURAGE** to re-aim yourself back towards **LIFE PLAN RIGHT**—in the wiser direction of soul-nurturing people, soul-nurturing values, soul-nurturing love.

Good news! This **COURAGE** to face up to that fleeting pain is well worth it. As my buddy Aristotle once said:

"Suffering becomes beautiful when anyone bears great calamities with cheerfulness, not through insensibility, but through greatness of mind."

Aristotle called this ability to withstand temporary pain for the greater good of gain of growth "**THE EDUCATION OF THE SOUL.**" According to Aristotle, every time you put in the effort to strengthen your soul just a wee bit more, you become just that wee bit happier. Aristotle also believed that even if someone is presently a "weak soul" they can be trained in the art of what he called "possessing the virtues of a strong character," because emotions involve beliefs, and beliefs are rational and educable.

THE BAD NEWS ABOUT EDUCATING THE SOUL:

Aristotle also recognized that our wishy-washy emotions often get lured in by tempting desires and somatic, subconscious factors. So, unfortunately merely wanting to change is not enough to promise change.

"But how is it that thought is sometimes followed by an action, sometimes not; sometimes by movement, sometimes not?" asked Aristotle.

THE ANSWER? Along with "virtue number one" of **COURAGE**, you also need to tap into "virtue number two" of **DISCIPLINE**.

Aristotle fully recognized that it takes **DISCIPLINE** to force yourself to move up, up, up on that less-crowded high road to **LIFE PLAN RIGHT** so as to become your **MIGHTIEST HUMAN BEING SELF**. Hence, why that hilly road to **LIFE PLAN RIGHT** is a less crowded road. However, Aristotle also recognized that once you start to put in the **DISCIPLINE** to go up, up, up those hills, it takes less effort over time, because soon traveling up the high road becomes a familiar habit. Soon you develop up-the-high-road-we-shall-go-muscle-groups to make the climb easier. In truth, the hardest part about that climb is to make the turnkey decision to climb.

"Virtue is a state of character concerned with choice," said Aristotle.

Yes, you always have a choice in life. It's always up to you to put in the **DISCIPLINE** and **COURAGE** needed to undergo the fleeting sting of **PAIN-A-RAMIC VISION** so you can become your **MIGHTIEST HUMAN BEING SELF**. It's always up to you to put in the **DISCIPLINE** and **COURAGE** to face up to your present **DESTRUCTIVE LOVE BELIEFS**, so you can once and for all morph them into **INSTRUCTIVE LOVE BELIEFS**—and thereby live happily ever after with a Prince Charming.

MY PROMISE:

If you right now choose to put in the **DISCIPLINE** and **COURAGE** to change your beliefs from **DESTRUCTIVE** to **INSTRUCTIVE** you will forever live happily ever after with a Prince Charming. Sounds good, right? Let's get started!

Coming up now I'm going to be giving you what I call **JACKHAMMER DRILLING QUESTIONS**—to help you dig deep, deep down into those dark subconscious caverns of your mind—where hidden

(b)lame excuses and false fears reside—all of the
DESTRUCTIVE LOVE BELIEFS that have created a very
limited version of the person you presently know
as *"That's Me!"* When you're done with doing these
JACKHAMMER DRILLING QUESTIONS I promise you
will emerge with a new, improved *"That's Me!"* one
which will let you become *your* **MIGHTIEST HUMAN
BEING SELF**—and snag a future living happily ever
after with a Prince Charming. Before we begin, I
want you to relax your mind. Breathe deeply. Enter
a meditative state. With each breath, I want you to
envision yourself breathing out fear, breathing in
love. When you feel calm, read on.

JACKHAMMER DRILLING QUESTIONS

*I. Who are you pissed off at for bringing you pain,
disappointment, failure, heartbreak? Go back in your
memory to as far as your childhood ... to last Tuesday.
I want you to write down each person's name—then
a brief description about the (b)lame excuses and
troublemaking fears that they have brought into
your life.* _____

_____

_____ .

*II. Are you riled up? Well, I'm gonna rile you up even
more. Next, I want you to look at your life with a full
"360-degree PAIN-A-RAMIC VISION" of your "That's
Me"—by asking you to answer the following questions:*

When it comes to love, I believe that _____

_____ .

I don't believe that _____

_____.

I blame my lack of love on _____

_____.

It's not my fault my love life sucks. It's because _____

_____

_____.

*I'm not the only one with a lousy love life. Many
people have lousy love lives because* _____

_____.

I fear _____

_____.

I hate _____

_____.

I love _____

_____.

I regret _____

_____.

I can't forgive _____

_____.

I resent _____

_____.

I envy _____

_____.

I feel it is impossible to find happy love because

_____

_____.

My childhood taught me when it comes to love to expect _____

_____.

Society taught me when it comes to love to expect ___

_____

_____.

The media taught me when it comes to love to expect

_____

_____.

I had a trauma/break up which taught me when it comes to love to expect _____

_____.

III. Now I want you to transform these beliefs from **DESTRUCTIVE** *to* **INSTRUCTIVE** *by taking the advice of positive psychology guru Martin Seligman—and creating "Positive Explanatory Stories" for all of the people you listed in question number one. Need help?*

a. Seligman suggests you become aware of using too much **"PERSONALIZATION."** *Meaning? You must have a healthy balance of internal blame vs. external blame in your storytelling. Were you at all self-responsible for any of the scenarios that unfolded? If not the original scenario, what about the* **REPETITION COMPULSION** *repeat performance scenarios? Brainstorm as many other interpretations as you can for what unfolded.*

_____

_____

_____

_____

_____

_____

_____

b. Seligman suggests you keep alert to **"PERVASIVE-NESS"** in your stories. In other words, do you believe this bad thing happened once—for a specific reason? Or did this bad thing happen due to universal causes—which means you're doomed for repeated torture—again and again? Find evidence to the contrary.

_____

_____

_____

_____

_____

c. Seligman suggests you watch out for describing your story with **"PERMANENCE."** For example, do you believe this bad thing had a temporary negative affect—or everlasting negative affect? How many times do you use **"ALWAYS"** and **"NEVER"** when you're telling your story? The goal: Rewrite your story without **"ALWAYS"** and **"NEVER."**

_____

_____

_____

_____

_____

_____

_____

_____

IV. Look at all your answers, and put all your **DESTRUCTIVE BELIEFS** *on trial—cross-examining each* **DESTRUCTIVE BELIEF** *like a tough attorney— until you can ably turn it into an* **INSTRUCTIVE BELIEF.** *Brainstorm new ways to dispute and discredit your (b)lame excuses—by gathering "positive evidence" to the contrary—coming up with proof of your lovability and the universe's abundance of happy love stories. Dispute and discredit your false fears by gathering lots of "contradictory evidence" about these fears—proving to yourself that your limited beliefs about your fears are just that—limited!*

_____

_____

_____

_____

_____

V. Pretend your life story is a made-up **FAIRY TALE STORY** *to be told to a little girl (maybe even* **YOU** *as a little girl). Now rewrite your life story so it has a happily ever after ending—by making sure the protagonist* **(YOU!)** *learns some mighty important life changing exciting lessons—which transform her into her* **(YOUR!) MIGHTIEST HUMAN BEING SELF!**

_____

_____

_____

_____

VI. Complete the following series of sentences:

Lucky, unlucky me, from this bad experience I learned

_____

_____ .

Lucky, unlucky me, from this bad experience I became
more _____

_____ .

Lucky, unlucky me, from this bad experience I met ___

_____

_____ .

Lucky, unlucky me, from this bad experience I
improved at being _____

_____ .

VII. I know it's a lot of fun to blame others for pain
and disappointments. But the good news is: If you
own your pain and disappointments, you can disown
them, too. So right now I want you to really face up
to your self-responsibility for what has happened in
your life. After all, you've been an adult or adult-ish
(and maybe even just plain ol' doltish) for a while
now. Although your troublemaking subconscious has
gotten you into some painful relationships, the time
has come for you to show your cerebrum who's boss
and stop allowing those painful misadventures, by

writing down how you know you contributed to your pain and disappointments.

_____

_____

_____

_____

_____

_____

_____

_____

VIII. Write down the names of family members you feel you can be open with about the concept of MASOCHISTIC EQUILIBRIUM. Now write down a time you plan to call them to talk openly about their CONSCIOUS INSIGHTS into your past—so you can gain even further CONSCIOUS INSIGHT.

_____

_____

_____

_____

_____

_____

_____

_____

_____

CONGRATULATIONS!

You have just taken lots of steps up that steep hill towards **LIFE PLAN RIGHT**—by putting in the **COURAGE** and **DISCIPLINE** to change your belief system.

REMEMBER:

You and you alone are the chooser of your beliefs! You are not your past history or past mistakes. You are only who you choose to believe you are here in this moment. You are only what you choose to do with your actions here in this moment! If you don't like what you've chosen so far in your past, you can rechoose right now in your present. Thanks to your answering these **JACKHAMMER DRILLING QUESTIONS,** you are well on your way to becoming a *choosier life choice chooser!*

In the next chapter I'm going to help you increase your womanly attraction—through the art of subtraction! You're going to be learning how to let go of lingering anger and resentment, which can tarnish your soul! Get ready to shine! A *sparkling, bling soul* shall soon be yours!

CHAPTER

5

The Law Of Attraction Begins With The Law Of Subtraction

(Forgiving Your Past Makes You More Sexy In Your Present)

ave you ever been to Mexico? For many years I used to visit Mexico for vacation—but found I kept getting sick. For a while I tried returning, promising myself next time I'd be smarter. I'd not only avoid the water, but anything with ice cubes. And no red meat. Unfortunately, no matter how careful I thought I was being, each time I still got sick. After a while I just did not want to go to Mexico anymore.

Experiencing a run of bad love relationships can become a lot like experiencing the runs in Mexico. If you keep feeling super bad, after a while you just don't want to travel to Love anymore. But you gotta have love in your life to be happy! It's in your human biological nature to need love (and sex!) to feel fully fulfilled and thriving. Aristotle also put this concept forth, explaining how we humans are *"biologically social animals."* He called love and friendship "essential external goods" of the highest importance—with insight and knowledge being "essential internal goods." Our true nature, according to Aristotle, is to love and be loved! Although, admittedly after a bad break up, the concept of experiencing love can feel more like *2,456,841st nature.*

I confess after I discovered my ex-Prince Harming was cheating, I was at first very tempted to just shut down and *Bonsai* myself—keeping myself emotionally protected from love. Thankfully I fought this urge, instead choosing to put in the **COURAGE** and **DISCIPLINE** to gather helpful **CONSCIOUS INSIGHTS** on love.

One of my first love lessons learned: *I had learned the wrong first love lesson!*

I was not meant to learn: *"I'll never fall in love again!"*

I was meant to learn: *"I didn't fully understand what true love was all about."*

Thanks to this ex-Prince Harming, I have gained a plethora of wonderful **CONSCIOUS INSIGHTS** on love—all of which have made me far wiser and happier—and led me into the arms of my now wonderful Prince Charming!

I even now look back on my ex-Prince Harming with gratitude for the love lessons learned because of him. So much so, I've re-nicknamed him my "Teacher." Literally. I jokingly call him this when I talk about him to friends. I even replaced his name in my cell phone as Teacher—so I'd be reminded of his role in my life.

And teach me he did! Thanks to this ex, I became determined to seek a **RELATIONSHIP OF SHARED VIRTUE** with my present Prince Charming. At this point in my life, I'm now even convinced that nearly all our lessons in life, are lessons in love. In fact, a big-time lesson in love is learning how to send loving thoughts to your ex—even if he has harmed you. You must compassionately understand that his "harming of you" is a sign of his inability to love rightly—because he is operating from a *lower consciousness*. You must therefore send your ex loving thoughts—pray for your ex to gain **CONSCIOUS INSIGHT** so he might grow into his **MIGHTIEST HUMAN BEING SELF.**

Yes, if you want to get better at loving and being loved, it's essential you learn the love of *compassionate forgiveness*. After all, it's super easy to send loving thoughts to someone who's being loving to you. But if you are to move forward into a healthful love relationship, you must first release the negative emotions from your past—all those lower vibrational energies created by anger, resentment and fears.

You must do this for many reasons. Let me start to explain by sharing a little story about a snake and a mistake.

THE SNAKE MISTAKE

There once was a woman who was wandering in the desert and got bitten by a poisonous snake. All she could think about was how angry she was at this poisonous snake for biting her, and angry at herself for wandering in the desert. And so she could not relax, forgive the snake, forgive herself, and thereby calmly see that she could solve this poison problem and save her life, simply by sucking out the poison from her arm, as she'd learned years ago—but forgotten because she was angry. She passed away. The lesson learned? Forgiveness is a panacea for what ails you.

It's funny. We all rationalize our anger as existing as a necessary force to impel us to better results. But more often than not, anger blocks us from our full mental clarity. Aristotle said it well when he said:

"We are easily deceived by our sense perceptions when we are in an emotional state . . . so that even a very slight resemblance makes the coward think that he sees his enemy . . . and the more emotional he is, the smaller is the similarity required to produce this effect."

Basically, it's in your best mental interests to release your anger at past relationships, so you can see the world more clearly around you.

Plus, anger is not only bad for your mental state, it's also unhealthy for your body, creating coronary heart disease, hypertension, stroke, high blood pressure and a compromised immune system. Angry people even take longer to recover from injury—as reported by researchers at the University of Ohio.

Anger has even been shown to be at the root of many addictions—as far ranging as drug, alcohol, food, and shopping addictions. According to psychologists, addicts seek these vices in order to avoid feeling the pain of past resentments. Their anger then becomes a boomerang—coming back to whack them with an addiction. A recent study performed by the University of Wisconsin even showed that **FORGIVENESS THERAPY** helped to relieve the anger behind substance abuse—even more successfully than routine drug/alcohol therapy. They did a test comparing **FORGIVENESS THERAPY** versus routine drug/alcohol therapy treatment. **FORGIVENESS THERAPY** not only showed faster success but created less recidivism.

Harboring hostility has also been linked with heart problems. One Yale study showed that when heart patients recalled a maddening event, their heart's electrical pulses started to beat madly. Suddenly they experienced a beat-to-beat EKG very similar to the irregular heartbeats of someone running at a fast speed on treadmill!

According to quantum physicists, angry thoughts give off electrical vibrations—literally creating electrical impulse changes within the brain—which can then literally change a person's vibrational field.

Basically, just as there is *alluring sexual attraction* (which people can feel but not see), there's also *angry energy repulsion* (which people can feel but not see). If you think angry thoughts, you will literally emit an angry vibration which can be intuitively felt by others—as if you're giving off an *anti-charisma*.

Many quantum physicists even believe your angry vibration can be felt in a larger universal energy field—thereby attracting negative circumstances.

Quantum physicists have reported many interesting studies about the powers of the positive and negative electrical impulses of the brain working almost like a broadcasting system. A well-known quantum physics expert, Lynne McTaggert, wrote about a study she witnessed where a happy person sent out loving energetic thoughts to an angry person—which then successfully calmed this angry person's temper.

Researcher Cleve Backster discovered that plants can sense when we are angry or happy. Backster attached electrode plates from a polygraph machine to a plant, then angrily imagined burning the plant's leaves with a match. As soon as this negative thought entered Backster's mind, the polygraph pen began move rapidly—as if the plant could fearfully sense what he was thinking.

I definitely believe it's not just plants that can sense angry, resentful energies. People can also sense if we're sending out loving energies or angry energies. For this reason I believe that **THE LAW OF ATTRACTION** (sending out sexy, loving vibrations into the world) must begin with **THE LAW OF SUBTRACTION** (letting go of negative energies like anger, resentment, fear).

Remember my **PRINCE CHARMING TRAIT#5?** I advised you to look for a happy person if you're to seek a happy relationship. Remember how I described how it's as if unhappy people give off *an unhappy smell.* Guess what? *You have to be the change you want to date!* You must make sure you're not giving off *an unhappy smell* because you're walking around thinking angry, resentful thoughts about your past partner—which your new partner can sense coming from you.

For all these many reasons, it's worth it to consciously put in the effort of forgiving and forgetting—so you can forge forward. Remember: *Anger remembered is anger relived—not relieved!*

The Law Of Subtraction (aka Forgiveness Therapy)

Begin by closing your eyes. Become aware of your breath. Tell yourself with every breath, you're breathing out anger, breathing in love. Breathe deeply from your diaphragm. Breathing from your chest won't relax you. If you want to add in an Aryuvedic breathing technique, you can also try putting a cotton ball in your right nostril and breathing only through the left nostril—which is promoted as helping to open up channels to the right brain and cool down anger.

I. Tell yourself: "I cannot always control what goes on outside. But I can always control what goes on inside. I forgive my ex, and am now determined to gain insights on how to wisely avoid love situations like this one in my future." Become determined to make this the breakup that led you to the breakdown that you led you to your breakthrough. Or as I also like to say: "Sometimes you have to reach "F*** this" to get to "Post-f*** this!"—that highly energized time when you are determined to break those damn patterns of pain.

Make this story about your Prince Harming become the story about how you stopped having Prince Harming Love Stories.

*II. Rename your ex as **"TEACHER"** to help you replace past anger with gratitude. Rewrite his name in your cell phone as **"TEACHER."** Trust me. You will feel so much better immediately.*

III. Write a Thank You Letter to your ex for all you've learned. Don't send it. Just keep it nearby—to read everytime you find yourself slipping back into your angry ways of thought.

IV. When angry feelings about your ex start to enter your mind, tell yourself about him: "We are all good, loving souls who occasionally get lost."

V. If you're still having trouble forgiving, remind yourself of a time you were forgiven. Decide to be altruistic, and forgive back to your ex.

VI. If you're continuing to have trouble forgiving, remind yourself that when you resent someone you are giving this person control of your emotions! And you don't want to give your ex that power!

VII. Still having trouble forgiving? Remind yourself that when you respond with hate-to-hate, anger-to-anger, bitterness-to-bitterness, you are ironically becoming part of the problem.

VIII. Forgiveness still not forthcoming? Remind yourself that when you train your brain to *consistently be more loving in its thoughts, your positive energy attracts more positive people and more positive results. Plus being peaceful within makes you far sexier—so you're more of a **LOVE MAGNET**. Ask yourself which you'd rather be: (1) A **NEGATIVITY MAGNET** — by thinking negative thoughts which attract negative circumstances? or (2) A* **LOVE MAGNET**—*by thinking loving thoughts which attract loving circumstances! I recommend the latter. Remember: Love success is the best revenge!*

Feeling better yet? I hope so! And I want to make sure you remain feeling peppy with love energy by getting you to become **TRIGGER HAPPY** on a daily basis—by triggering happy thoughts within you as often as possible. How?

DAILY TRIGGER HAPPY TIPS

I. Walk around your home, removing potentially negative triggers from your past (depressing photos, gifts, notes, etc.) which could cascade you downwards into feelings of pain, anger, regret.

II. Put out positive triggers (happy photos, gifts, notes, etc.) that remind you of all the love you have in your life with family and friends.

*III. Create the utmost **TRIGGER HAPPY** item: **A LOVE VISION BOARD**.*

Have you ever heard of **A LOVE VISION BOARD?** It's a super fun and empowering method for creating a literal visual form of a visualization. **A LOVE**

VISION BOARD is easy to make. Page through a pile of magazines, cutting out images that represent what you desire and expect in your new soon-to-be snagged *Happily Ever After Love Future.* Paste these images onto a large piece of cardboard you can buy at an art supply store. After you're done having fun pasting up these images, stare at this fabulous work of **VISION BOARD** art as often as possible.

I'm a big believer that seeing your visualization come to life like this absolutely serves to effectively reach more nooks and crannies of your brain and heart than ordinary closed-eye visualizations! I'm also very confident Aristotle would enthusiastically approve of your creating this fun and effective **VISION BOARD** art project —for many reasons.

Firstly, Aristotle was a big fan of the arts—for both its inspirational and cathartic benefits. On this account, Aristotle was very different from Plato, who in contrast, badmouthed art—calling it an *"inferior appeal to human emotions."* Plato basically argued that art is a representation of mere appearances— and thereby was misleading, morally suspect and dangerous to society. Plato even went so far as to recommend that poets, writers—artists in general— all be banished because they served no ethical utility.

Meaning Plato wouldn't be so apt to join me—a professional writer—for a frappuccino at Starbucks— even if I asked him nicely and offered to treat! Plato was concerned that if an art form—say, a play which was a tragedy—represented something dark and depressing—after seeing it, you'd leave the theater feeling bummed. And if the art form was a happy love story play—representing a high ideal— you'd leave the theater equally as bummed—because you'd feel your life didn't match up with this ideal. *According to Plato,* **ART=DANGER.**

Aristotle—in contrast—loved the idea of artists wandering our planet—or seated at tables hunched over their laptops in Starbucks — because Aristotle believed art was nurturing to the soul—so much so, he believed art was even a step or two higher in importance than history!

"The distinction between historian and poet is not in the one writing prose and the other verse," said Aristotle. "You might put the work of Herodotus into verse, and it would still be a species of history; it consists really in this ... that the one describes the thing that has been, and the other a kind of thing that might be. Hence poetry is something more philosophic and of graver import than history, since its statements are of the nature rather of universals, whereas those of history are singular."

Basically, Aristotle believed art stimulated the soul because it encouraged the soul to seek more from life—seek new possibilities. Hence why I'm confident that Aristotle would love the concept of a **VISION BOARD**—because it's a form of art with the specific purpose of stimulating the soul to pursue the fabulous ideals it represents!

Aristotle was also a big believer that *"making an art form"* was just as nurturing to the soul as *"watching an art form."* He recognized that creativity was not only crucial to the growth of kids, but adults, too.

THINK ABOUT IT.

Only we humans have this creativity perk. It's one of our unique human skill sets—up there with our unique human perk to tap into **CONSCIOUS INSIGHT**. Hence you as a human owe it to yourself to cash in on your ability to both *"create art"* and *"experience art"*—so as to achieve becoming your **MIGHTIEST HUMAN BEING SELF.**

Aristotle also loved that art could be a big-time stimulator of **CONSCIOUS INSIGHT**—because art could snap you out of your humdrum mundane daily rituals.

IT'S LIKE THIS:

When you experience art—unlike when you experience your humdrum mundane daily rituals— you are roused by your startled sensations from your sleepwalking-thru-life tendencies—thereby exciting your human perk of **CONSCIOUS INSIGHT**. Art thereby becomes *A Great Unconcealer*—awakening you to see more and feel more—so you feel more truly alive and thriving. Art shakes you up and wakes you up—arousing higher levels of insights—which then fuel your growth and happiness.

Aristotle even admitted that he saw one humongous benefit to *"experiencing the arts"* that even philosophy—his pet field of interest—did not offer people. *"For philosophy, 'seeing' is contemplation, while for the arts it is CATHARSIS,"* said Aristotle.

WHAT IS CATHARSIS EXACTLY?

A Greek word literally meaning "to cleanse." It's all about releasing trapped emotions.

HOW IS IT THAT CATHARSIS WORKS VIA ART?

"Art awakens in the soul the ideal type of reality, and hence, rather than stir up the passions, frees the soul from disturbances (CATHARSIS) which have their origin in the passions," said Aristotle.

MEANING? Art gets under your skin and deep into your heart—digging down into unexplored places where you've buried negative emotions. Then art rouses up this **"CATHARSIS"**—this emotional release—by rattling up your soul to focus on what it needs to act on—riling up your soul to grow to reach new ideals—to aim you more clearly towards **LIFE PLAN RIGHT**.

Yes, keeping in mind all of art's rousing, rattling and riling abilities, I'm very confident Aristotle would approve of you creating and using a **VISION BOARD**—so as to rouse, rattle and rile you to stay aimed rightly toward living happily ever after in love with a Prince Charming.

Personally, I'm a big believer that pain from the past persists— until a strong enough vision for superior times replaces it. By creating a **VISION BOARD**, you can more easily forgive your past, because you know by letting go of what was, you can make room for a far, far better will be!

After you're done cutting and pasting together a gorgeous **VISION BOARD**, hurry up and meet me in Chapter 6 for some seduction tips that will make your new Prince Charming putty in your nimble hands.

CHAPTER

6

Be The Change You Want To Date

(If You Wanna Snag A Prince Charming,
You Must Become A Princess Charming)

Have you noticed the fancy shmancy juice choices that are out there today? They have things like:

Get Smart Juice
Passion Power
Memory Master

But nobody makes juices like . . .

Niceness Nectar
Consideration Cocktail
Generosity Frappucino
Good Listener Smoothie

Interesting, eh? No manufacturer bothers to make any juices that offer up the potential for building a stronger character or a bigger heart—which is what truly improves lives most!

At first when I noticed this I thought how maybe manufacturers just can't make those juices. But— I'm betting if manufacturers knew there was money to be made from these *"strong character building"* juices, they would find a way to produce 'em!

Manufacturers probably just figure nobody would buy juices which make you nicer, more considerate, more generous or a better listener—because working to strengthen these character values is just not valued enough in this world!

What a shame! I believe the lack of emphasis on improving these character values is exactly what is creating many of the problems in our world at large—and your present love life.

Let me explain. As I mentioned earlier, Aristotle was a big believer that it's worth it to be a good person—even in a bad world—because being a good person—with good character values—is what aims you down that happy path to the best kind of love (**RELATIONSHIP OF SHARED VIRTUE**) and the best kind of happiness (becoming your **MIGHTIEST HUMAN BEING SELF).**

If you weakly misbehave by indulging in too many immediate pleasures in too much of an extreme (drinking too many dirty martinis, pigging out on too much chocolate, over-shopping for too many shoes, dating souldmate hottie Prince Harmings who are bad boys) you will be heading foolishly towards **LIFE PLAN WRONG.** As a result, you won't be able to reach your actual true ends of happiness— heading towards **LIFE PLAN RIGHT**—towards living happily ever after with your Prince Charming. For this reason, Aristotle offered up a big secret to happiness:

DO ACTIONS YOU ARE PROUD OF!

Aristotle firmly put forth that it's highly worth it to be a good person! *You must become the change you want to see and date!* Yes—if you want to lure in a Prince Charming, you must live up to being worthy of snagging one!

IT'S LIKE THIS:

You might think you can get away with being naughty not nice—but your soul will always know when you misbehave. Your soul will always know the truth about what you are doing—or not doing—even if nobody else knows. It's as if your soul is *a constant candid camera* recording the reality of your life wherever you go. And if you're naughty too often—you will become an unhappy person with low self-esteem—and thereby you will not become *Worthy Prince Charming Bait!* Listen up! Aristotle said it well when he said:

"Dignity consists not in possessing honors, but in the consciousness that we deserve them."

MEANING? There is no way to dupe your soul— hence it's highly worthwhile to consistently choose morally right actions your soul can be proud of!

ARISTOTLE'S #1 SECRET FOR HAPPINESS: BE GODDAMN VIRTUOUS!

Unfortunately, here in America this big secret for happiness seems to be remaining a big secret. Too many people have sold their souls! With these *soulds* of theirs, they are overly valuing power, beauty, fame, status, money, money, money! *(Note: Did I mention money?)* Yes, there are far too many people with soulds who are out there seeking instantaneous indulgence gratification in the form of overeating, drugging, cheating in business, cheating in love, winning at any/all costs.

The cost these people with *soulds* are paying is a high one: unfulfilling love lives, low self-esteem and rampant depression!

Aristotle was a big believer that every time you behaved immorally—performing actions your soul was not proud of—*you tarnished your sould.* The worst shape your soul became in—the worst shape your mood and spirit. Basically, you cannot be a happy person if you don't nurture your soul with actions your soul can be proud of! The larger and more frequent your unsoulful acts (i.e., being unkind, ungenerous, inconsiderate, immoral) *the more tarnished your sould*—and the larger and deeper your sadness.

IN SUMMARY:

Although you might think you can get away with being unkind, ungenerous, inconsiderate and immoral—you can never lie to your soul.

In my opinion, this bad *sould* versus good soul theory of happiness is why Prozak and Zoloft don't truly work long-term on many people—that is people without true chemical imbalances.

IT'S LIKE THIS:

If you take these happiness pills, and don't change your life for the soul-nurturing better, you're simply making superficial changes in your brain chemistry. Prozak and Zoloft might be able to temporarily fool your brain chemistry into believing you are a happy person. Unfortunately, Prozak and Zoloft do not work on your soul! Unless you start to create major soul-nurturing life changes while on these happiness pills, you will remain an unhappy person.

GOOD NEWS FOR GOOD PEOPLE

Aristotle believed that a person with a strong good soul—*who possesses the virtues of character*—will always more resiliently recover from bad experiences far faster and easier than a badly behaving person of weak character—weak *sould*—for the same reason that a physically in-shape person will more easily recover from a car accident than an out of shape person. The person who possesses the virtues of character is intrinsically emotionally and spiritually stronger.

WANT PROOF? HOW ABOUT OPRAH. Here is a woman who was raped at a young age—but intrinsically possesses the virtues of character and thereby now possesses the admiration of gazillions and has definitely aimed herself towards **LIFE PLAN RIGHT!**

In contrast, I believe America's rampant Prozak-popping depression is due to so many people lying, cheating, pillaging their way to the top penthouse apartment—all in hopes of finding nirvanic happiness—otherwise known as *fleeting pleasure*—which translates into a fool's paradise!

I SAID IT BEFORE AND I'LL SAY IT AGAIN: In order to be happy, you must tap into the **COURAGE** and **DISCIPLINE** needed to become your **MIGHTIEST HUMAN BEING SELF**. And it's not enough to just be a good person every once in a while. You gotta learn to live daily in this place of strong character. As Aristotle warned:

"One swallow does not a spring make – and one swallow of Slimfast does not a successful diet make."

Or at least he said half of that expression! His point was that you gotta keep doing the good thing to earn out the positive rewards of the good thing – and to earn out being considered a good person. To quote Aristotle—precisely this time:

"Thus, it is not enough to perform one act of generosity in order to be generous; it is necessary to act constantly according to the dictates of reason."

Aristotle admitted that constancy of a habit can be used both for you—or against you.

I. You can pick a nice habit of virtue to embrace— so as to become a good person of virtue: a kind, considerate, generous, good listener.

II. You can pick a favorite naughty vice to make your very own so as to become a jerk: a self-centered, dishonest, lazy, mean scoundrel.

It's your choice which virtues you choose to make your own. And through the choices in virtues you ultimately embrace—*naughty versus nice*—you will either wind up being blessed with soul-nurtured happy love—or cursed with a constant dull wave of sadness due to *your weak tarnished sould*—settling for being with a souldmate Prince Harming.

THE ADMITTED PROBLEM:

Often we humans make decisions in the moment— about which habits to choose—without thinking about long-term consequences.

THE HAPPY SOLUTION:

We humans have that unique human perk— **CONSCIOUS INSIGHT**—which is a powerful protector against us deciding to behave naughty or nice.

THE ADMITTED PROBLEM ABOUT THIS HAPPY SOLUTION:

As I mentioned earlier, tapping into this unique human superpower of **CONSCIOUS INSIGHT** also means tapping into **COURAGE** and **DISCIPLINE**. Many average people don't want to tap into **COURAGE** and **DISCIPLINE**. Luckily you are not average! You are a **MIGHTY HUMAN BEING SELF**— *a Princess Charming!* You recognize the long-term

benefits of tapping into **COURAGE** and **DISCIPLINE**—
so you can keep on growing—and growing—into
your *Absolute Mightiest Princess Charming Self!*

THE LONG-TERM BENEFITS OF BEING A GOOD, STRONG SOUL

I. You will be happier.
II. You will be sexier.
III. You will have higher self-esteem.
*IV. You will be strong enough to resist the lure of a
souldmate Prince Harming*
*V. You will feel as if you are a worthy soul who
deserves to love and be loved by a soulmate Prince
Charming—and Prince Charmings will want you!*

The world is your mirror. People tend to attract the
people and circumstances they believe themselves
worthy of attracting!

Unfortunately, many women walk around operating
from an unconscious autopilot mind, thinking:

*"I deserve a great happy love relationship with a
Prince Charming."*

Meanwhile, in their subconscious minds, these
women don't feel worthy of a great love happy relationship—because their *candid camera soulds* have
watched them misbehaving as a Princess Harming—
not as a Princess Charming. Plus, even if a Princess
Harming gal manages to temporarily trick a Prince
Charming guy into being with her—eventually her
weak tarnished sould will perform actions that self-

sabotage the love of her Prince Charming—due to her operating from that previously mentioned **MASOCHISTIC EQUILIBRIUM** tendency.

I want you to take some time now to tap into your fab human perk of **CONSCIOUS INSIGHT** and ask yourself:

Are you being nice, considerate, warmly communicative, a good listener, patient, generous, loving, empathic?

You have to get your identity in order if you want your love life to be in order! You have to fully believe in your soul that you are being your **MIGHTIEST HUMAN BEING SELF**—*a Princess Charming*—if you want to head towards a good happy love life with a Prince Charming.

Your identity is the chooser of your actions and habits!

Your identity = your destiny

FOR A QUICKIE EXAMPLE:

If you're not a good listener—nor are you empathic—then you will behave badly with your man—and your love life will suffer.

For this reason, I believe it's important to write a **TO BE LIST** first thing in the morning—even before you write your **TO DO LIST**. After all, who you think you are will affect how well you get your **TO DO LIST** done—and determine what items you choose as top value items to do on your **TO DO LIST**. Frank Sinatra sang: **"DO BE DO BE DO."** Frank's a great crooner—

but he's a dyslexic self-help guru. To live your happiest life, you gotta sing: **"BE DO BE DO BE DO."** You have to put emphasis on **BEING** before **DOING.**

FOR ANOTHER QUICKIE EXAMPLE:

If you are being a kind, honest, loving, patient, communicative, loyal person—as a result you will then be doing kind, honest, loving, patient, communicative actions!

With this in mind, a hugely important question to keep asking yourself is:

"Who do you need to become to get all which you want in your life?"

I love this question. You can solve a lot of the problems in your life by asking yourself this question, then finding the right **TO BE LIST** words to focus on being more of *(i.e., patient, disciplined, courageous, forgiving)*—so as to amend your problematic areas.

ANOTHER QUICKIE EXAMPLE:

If you realize you have a weakness in being able to be a *"warmly direct"* woman—and thereby you're not being honest with your partner—you need to put *"warmly direct"* on your **TO BE LIST.** If you realize you're not a *"good listener"*—and so your partner feels unheard and annoyed—you need to put *"good listener"* on your **TO BE LIST.** Hence why every morning you must start your day by thinking about that question:

"Who do you need to become to get all which you want in your life?"

Or if you want, you can even narrow-focus the question to become:

"Who do you need to become to get the happy love life and Prince Charming you want in your life?"

Start your morning by writing up your **TO BE LIST**—and really think about being those **TO BE'S**! If you're tempted to not be those **TO BE'S**, immediately repeat the following mantra:

"The old me used to be that way, the new me isn't, dammit!"

ANOTHER QUICKIE EXAMPLE:

"The Old Me used to be very reactive and say things without thinking in the moment. The New Me calms down before speaking, so I'm responding, not reacting."

By constantly repeating, *"The old me used to be that way, the new me isn't, dammit!"* you can absolutely train your brain to hold a new identity about yourself as your **MIGHTIEST PRINCESS CHARMING SELF**— and thereby create new, different, better love life options!

Next up, let me share a bit more about how to create the best **TO BE LIST**—a la my favorite philosopher buddy, Aristotle.

Aristotle believed that the all of life can be arranged into what he called a **"TRIAD."** On one side there is excess. On the other, its extreme deficiency. And in between is a little something he recommended being— which he called **"THE MEAN."** In life, **"THE MEAN"** always equals the "good strong character value."

FOR A QUICKIE EXAMPLE:

In between fearfulness and rashness is the mean of **COURAGE**. In between stinginess and lavishness is the mean of generosity.

Aristotle believed everything has a **MEAN ZONE**—all of life's actions, feelings and material goods.

Even love has a **MEAN ZONE**! It exists somewhere between coldness and co-dependent suffocation.

Even truth has a **MEAN ZONE**! It exists somewhere between outright lying and being hurtfully direct.

Even niceness has a **MEAN ZONE**! It exists somewhere between being a spineless worm and a jerk.

MEANING? If sometimes you haven't been attracted to a guy because he's *"too nice!"*—you were intuitively correct for not being attracted. It's not *"strong character"* to be spineless, wormy, too nice. Guess what? You too must watch out for being spineless wormy too nice with a guy. After all . . .

It's hard to be your prettiest self when you have footprints on your face!

If you want to be a good, consciously insightful strong soul—*a Princess Charming who attracts a Prince Charming*—you must choose to live your life in this **MEAN ZONE**—even when bad experiences happen that make you feel angry. And good souls— even Princess Charmings and Prince Charmings —will feel anger. The goal is to feel anger rightly—in this **MEAN ZONE**! Hence Aristotle's ditty:

"Anybody can become angry—that is easy, but to be angry with the right person and to the right degree and at the right time and for the right purpose, and in the right way—that is not within everybody's power and is not easy."

When Aristotle wrote this, he was admitting how it's very human to feel negative emotions at times. It's very okay to feel anger, hurt, sadness—as long as you tame your emotions with rational reason, keeping your feelings in the **MEAN ZONE**—where human passion is tamed by that human perk of **CONSCIOUS INSIGHT**! Aristotle also simultaneously warned that whenever a person lives with any pleasure in the **EXTREME ZONE**, he's bound to hurt himself and others.

A QUICKIE EXAMPLE:

If you put an overemphasis on money, sex, power, fame, beauty, food, drugs—you're making this *"value"* more important than the *"higher good value"* of becoming your **MIGHTIEST PRINCESS CHARMING SELF**. Not only will you not be fully happy—but your lack of disciplined character could easily lead to your harming others. Hence why you should avoid Prince Harmings who live their lives overly-valuing sex, overly-valuing money, overly-valuing status, overly-valuing power, overly-valuing beauty—putting these "values" in an **EXTREME ZONE**—because eventually you'll have to endure their **WEAK CHARACTER VALUES SIDE EFFECTS**.

2 QUICKIE EXAMPLES:

I. Prince Harmings who *overly value sex* will cheat on you.

II. Prince Harmings who *overly value beauty* will dump you if you gain ten pounds.

A QUICKIE REMINDER:

If right now you find yourself with an extreme urge for sex, money, shoes, beauty—any superficial now, now, now immediate pleasure—then this extreme urge thing might dangerously get in your way of becoming your highest potential Princesss Charming self and . . . well, you will find yourself *living UN-happily ever after*.

Basically you must learn to live a life using "moderation" as your measurement tool for how much you indulge in a feeling or a habit. If you find you are presently feeling an emotion or doing a habit in an extreme zone, you must put in the virtue of

DISCIPLINE to tame this feeling and/or habit so you get it nestled in the **MEAN ZONE**.

For example, if right now you are feeling fearful about love, then you need to really do some inner work around the **TO BE** word of "courageous." But while you are doing this **TO BE** work on being "courageous," you must make sure you do not develop an excessive sense of courage by becoming rash—which is a vice! The true virtue of "courageous" is nestled within **THE MEAN ZONE** of the excessive extreme vice of rashness and the deficient extreme vice of cowardice. Below is a quickie chart with some more examples.

What it Means To Live Within "THE MEAN"

VICE OF DEFICIENCY	VIRTUOUS MEAN	VICE OF EXCESS
Cowardice	Courage	Rashness
Insensibility	Temperance	Intemperance
Pettiness	Munificence	Vulgarity
Humble-mindedness	High-mindedness	Vaingloriness
Want of Ambition	Right Ambition	Over-ambition
Spiritlessness	Good Temper	Irascibility
Surliness	Friendly Civility	Obsequiousness
Ironical Depreciation	Sincerity	Boastfulness
Boorishness	Wittiness	Buffoonery
Shamelessness	Modesty	Bashfulness
Callousness	Just Resentment	Spitefulness

IN SUMMARY:

You must consciously strive to become the change you want to date—which brings us back to that list of 5 traits I assigned you to look for in your Prince Charming! You must work on embracing these 5 traits within yourself as well—if you ever want to *live happily ever after with a Prince Charming!*

The 5 Traits You Need To Embrace To Become A Princess Charming:

Princess Charming Trait #1: Do you want to be married and have kids? (If so, stick to this value when you are out there choosing a partner. Be disciplined about dating men who do not share these values for a relationship!)

*Princess Charming Trait #2: Do you value growing as a person? (Are you striving to live a life in that **"MEAN ZONE"** of good soul behavior? Do you value wanting to become your highest potential—owning self-responsibility and seeking insights?)*

*Princess Charming Trait #3: Do you understand that a relationship serves 2 functions? It's not solely a **"DEN FOR PLEASURE"**—it's also a soul's **"LABORATORY FOR GROWTH."** (Basically, do you embrace values which show you absolutely want a **"RELATIONSHIP OF SHARED VIRTUE"**?)*

Princess Charming Trait #4: Do you make your partner feel "safe" in the relationship to be his fullest potential? (Do you lose your temper, show contempt/ judgment, lie, cheat, act inconsistently? Stop it! You need to create a safe environment for your partner, so he feels he can be vulnerable enough for true intimacy!)

*Princess Charming Trait #5: Are you a happy person? (Have you released your anger from your past relationships and childhood disappointments? Do you do actions you are proud of—so you have high self-esteem? Are you feeling emotions in the "**MEAN ZONE**" and being the Princess Charming well-behaved person you most want to be —so you feel super happy about being you? Are you addiction-free?)*

After reading these 5 traits, how do you feel? I want you to really think about these 5 traits, then take some time to answer that super important question I asked you earlier. Here's that question again:

"Who do you need to become to get all that you want in your life?"

Or if you want, narrow-focus the question to become this:

"Who do you need to become to get the happy love life and Prince Charming you want in your life?"

Write what you now want to grow within yourself here . . .

_____

_____

_____

_____

_____

_____

_____

REMEMBER:

You must grow yourself if you want to grow your entire life. As Aristotle admitted, this self-growth requires you embracing specific virtues:

I. COURAGE
II. DISCIPLINE
III. CONSISTENCY OF HABIT

Oh—and let me throw in one more toughie virtue:

IV. PATIENCE

Yes, unfortunately, although you might be making internal changes within yourself quickly, the external changes in your life might take longer to manifest—in the same way that planted seeds need time to grow. Ditto on your new thought seeds, new belief seeds, and new habit seeds! All these new seeds will take time to manifest into the change you are seeking. Hence, during this time of striving for self-change, it's important you keep reassuring yourself that what you see with your limited short-term lens is not necessarily what you are getting in your long–term future. During this time, it's important to keep yourself focused on the long–term benefits of your self-growth efforts—by staring at your **VISION BOARD** and re-reading your *happily ever after **LOVE VISUALIZATION***. I'm a big believer in the following:

INCREASE YOUR WHYPOWER
TO INCREASE YOUR WILLPOWER

The more you believe in **WHY** you must be courageous, disciplined, consistent and patient—the more **WILLPOWER** you will have to put in this **COURAGE, DISCIPLINE, CONSISTENCY** and **PATIENCE.**

Want another willpower tip? Memorize the following:

SEEING IS NOT ALWAYS BELIEVING.
HOWEVER SEEDING IS BELIEVING.
WHAT YOU SEED IS WHAT YOU GET.

If you are seeding positive thoughts and positive actions, you can feel certain that overtime success will eventually blossom! You can feel certain that your You Seed—Your **ENTELECHY**—will grow into its **MIGHTIEST HUMAN BEING SELF!**

Also, keep in mind that if you occasionally fall off **THE DISCIPLINE WAGON** as you head up, up, up that high road to **LIFE PLAN RIGHT**, do not worry. It's normal to be human and fall off **THE DISCIPLINE**

WAGON on occasion. As you climb back onto your **DISCIPLINE WAGON**, keep in mind the following ditty from Aristotle:

"Moreover, this remains true, no matter how virtuous we become, for passion is like a wild beast and anger perverts rulers even when they are the best men."

Meaning, hey, we humans are all human—and human temptation is everywhere. So, add these words onto your **TO BE LIST**:

to be self-forgiving
to be focused on persistence not perfection

By the way—it's actually good news if you call off **A DISCIPLINE WAGON**—because it means you at least have **A DISCIPLINE WAGON** to fall off of—and you're on your way to *change!* Yay you!

Speaking of change ... many women think they have to change the way they look to attract a Prince Charming. I'm a big believer that beauty is not only in the eyes of the beholder, but the ears and heart of the beholder. Coming up in the next chapter, I will explain why learning the secrets of **PRINCESS CHARMING SCHOOL** is far more important than any secrets you might learn in **BEAUTY SCHOOL**!

CHAPTER

7

Princess Charming School Secrets For Seduction

(Far More Alluring Than Beauty School Secrets)

Back in Ancient Greece, the word "school" also meant "leisure," because so much leisure time was devoted to learning—unlike here in America today. Here in Modern America, it's unfortunately getting more and more rare for folks to read and study in leisure time. We've become a nation of narrow-focused specialists, with scant time to learn anything outside our chosen professions.

According to Aristotle, this **LIMITED STIMULATION MIND DIET** is bad for the soul—which is constantly hungry for stimulus from the outside world. Or to quote my soul-mate philosopher Aristotle directly:

"The soul is characterized by these capacities: self-nutrition, sensation, thinking and movement."

MEANING? The more you caretake your soul with all four of these **FOUR BASIC FEED-YOUR-SOUL GROUPS,** the happier and perkier your soul will be. And the more you can caretake your partner's soul with these **FOUR BASIC FEED-YOUR-SOUL GROUPS,** the happier your partner's soul will be—and the more deeply he will truly connect with you and love you!

Most relationships end because of daily **BOREDOM.
EVEN SEXUAL BOREDOM**—which actually comes
more from **MENTAL AND EMOTIONAL BOREDOM**
than it does from **WE NEED TO FIND NEW SEXUAL
POSITIONS BOREDOM.** Where does all this
BOREDOM come from, you ask? Lack of stimulation
of the soul!

Remember how in Chapter 1 I said Aristotle would
believe that the soul is the real *g-spot for happiness?*
Well, it's true. When you can grab a man by his
soul—truly turn on a man's soul—then and only
then will this man be your Prince Charming who
desires to live happily ever after with you.

Unfortunately, if you only know how to grab a
man by his-you-know-what—then you will only
be attracting him sexually, and he will get bored
eventually and move on.

When You Only Know
How To Grab A Man By
His-You-Know-What,
You Are Only In:

I. A RELATIONSHIP OF PLEASURE—a union based on
your being his sex, drugs and rock 'n roll partner!

II. RELATIONSHIP OF UTILITY—a union based on
your being his ego's arm candy partner!

LISTEN UP!

If you can't stimulate your Prince Crush in more areas than the waist down, he will not remain your Prince Crush for long.

One of my favorite quotes about love comes from the book *The Little Prince:*

"It's only with the heart that one can see rightly; what's most important is invisible to the eye."

I love that the Little Prince recognized that the heart (another metaphysical word for "soul") makes the best lens for love—making this Little Prince a Major Prince Charming.

TO SUM IT UP

If you want to be a man's Princess Charming, you must tap into what I call **THE SCHEHERAZADE EFFECT**. Remember the tale of Scheherazade and her 1001 nights? Scheherazade was absolutely a Princess Charming who knew how to grab and stimulate her King's soul. I can promise you that if you use the secrets of the captivating Scheherazade—you will develop deeper, more long-lasting love—a **RELATIONSHIP OF SHARED VIRTUE**.

THE "CLIFF NOTES" ON SCHEHERAZADE

There once was a King who got very bored with the women in his life very quickly. He would marry a new virgin, "shtup" her, then send her pretty self away pretty much immediately—to be beheaded. Talk about a bad breakup, huh? And talk about a King Harming, huh? Anyway, this King killed thousands of women by the time he finally met the enchantingly different Scheherazade. What made Scheherazade enchantingly different? Scheherazade loved to read books, and had lots of fascinating ideas and interests to share. She had a passion for poetry, philosophy, sciences, arts—and was wisely educated in morality and kindness. Basically, Scheherazade was loving, smart, witty, well-read and well-bred. She kept the King on the edge of his bed—not with mere alluring sexual positions—but with alluring stories to be told—each more exciting than the next. And so the King kept Scheherazade alive—eagerly anticipating each new tale—until, lo and behold—one thousand and one adventurous nights passed—along with three sons—and the King not only learned to love Scheherazade—he made her his Queen. Talk about living happily ever after, huh?

THE LESSON LEARNED?

It's very seductive to a man when you as a full-bodied and full soul-ed Princess Charming have passions in your life you can share with him and keep him inspired and titillated and growing and thriving. Indeed the more passions you have in your life, the more passion your man will have for you! Plus it's very appealing if you have One Specific Passion in your life that excites your soul—or what Aristotle called **"YOUR UNIQUE SPECIFIC FUNCTION."**

Aristotle believed for you to grow into your **MIGHTIEST HUMAN BEING SELF**, you had to find your soul's **UNIQUE SPECIFIC FUNCTION**—and then do it—or your soul would be unhappy. Aristotle said it well when he said:

"Man is a goal-seeking animal. His life only has meaning if he is reaching out and striving for his goals."

Aristotle went on to describe **YOUR UNIQUE SPECIFIC FUNCTION** as the very special thing which excites *your* **ENTELECHY**—*your You Seed*—the special thing which only you can do—and you can do better than anyone else.

WHAT'S YOUR UNIQUE SPECIFIC FUNCTION?

The function of a physician is to heal.
The function of a ship builder is to build great ships.
The function of a shoemaker is to make great shoes (preferably Christian Laboutins).
The function of a mom is to be a mom.
The function of you is to _____ ?

When I first read about this concept of **YOUR UNIQUE SPECIFIC FUNCTION**, I immediately knew my own: *"To write books that inspire people."* And writing self-help books like this one you are holding is definitely working to keep me happy.

I've always been alert to the connection between *"the pursuit of happiness"* and *"the pursuit of a* **UNIQUE SPECIFIC FUNCTION***"*—or what I called

"A Dream Quest" in my book *ENOUGH, DAMMIT.* A big belief of mine is:

The purpose of your life is to find and do the purpose of your life.

For the last decade I've been coaching clients to live a life that includes a passionate purpose. Having coached an infinite number of people by now, I have proven/reproven/re-re-proven that the happiest folks are always those pursuing their unique-to-them passion, either for a living—or even a la carte on the evenings and weekends as a hobby. Not surprisingly, the unhappiest folks are those who feel trapped in an unfulfilling job or lifestyle—who complain they never have time to indulge in their favorite passions even as a hobby a la carte to their job.

The highly famed and revered psychologist Abraham Maslow also preached the importance of pursuing a **UNIQUE SPECIFIC FUNCTION** in order to feel fulfilled. As Maslow said:

"Musicians must make music, artists must paint, poets must write if they are to be ultimately at peace with themselves. What human beings can be, they must be. They must be true to their own nature. This need we may call self-actualization. It refers to man's desire for self-fulfillment, namely to the tendency for him to become actually in what he is potentially: to become everything one is capable of becoming."

Basically, Maslow agreed with Aristotle on how important the need to grow is to being happy.

The famed and revered psychologist Carl Jung also "ditto-ed" this sentiment about the essentialness of pursuing **YOUR UNIQUE SPECIFIC FUNCTION.** Jung even had a dating warning about what happens if you do not pursue it.

Carl Jung's Dating Warning About Not Pursuing your Unique Specific Function:

*Jung believed that your life needs meaning and purpose if you are to be happy—what he referred to as **A SPIRITUAL QUEST** (which is his lingo for **YOUR UNIQUE SPECIFIC FUNCTION**, A Dream Quest , A Major Passion—whatever you want to call it). If you don't have a **HIGH-LEVEL SPIRITUAL QUEST** that brings you meaning and purpose, you will acquire a **LOW-LEVEL SPIRITUAL QUEST** in the form of "a bad habit," "a major conflict," an "addiction"—or you'll desire "Prince Harming Highly Painful Relationships"—in* order to create needed drama and excitement.

THE GOOD NEWS:

You can more readily stop indulging in a **LOW-LEVEL SPIRITUAL QUEST** like dating Prince Harmings by developing a **HIGH-LEVEL SPIRITUAL QUEST / UNIQUE SPECIFIC FUNCTION**—a driving positive force that propels you forward.

MEANING? Often, it's easier to dump **LOW-LEVEL SPIRITUAL QUEST** negative patterns in love if you replace them with something else that brings you purpose and excitement—like cycling, skydiving, scuba diving, exotic cooking, ceramics, tennis. Who knows … maybe in the process, you'll find a **HIGH-LEVEL SPIRITUAL QUEST** Prince Charming—who'll share your stimulating new hobby! Even if your Prince Charming doesn't share your exact interest in your **HIGH-LEVEL SPIRITUAL QUEST/ UNIQUE SPECIFIC FUNCTION**—he will find you far more interesting because you have a passion (or a lot of them). Any which way, simply doing this **HIGH-LEVEL SPIRITUAL QUEST** will make you wildly seductive to men everywhere. Our world is full of love stories peppered with women who were not "perfect looking" on the outside—but who were so fascinating and thrilling to be around, men were hypnotized by them.

Another major reason why doing your **HIGH-LEVEL SPIRITUAL QUEST** makes you wildly attractive: It raises your *self-esteem.* You're less focused on whether or not you look perfect on the outside, when you feel amazing on your inside. And *"self–love"* is essential if you are to love and be loved by another.

Aristotle was a big fan of self-love. He even believed it to be the very first condition to achieve the highest form of love—a **RELATIONSHIP OF SHARED VIRTUE.** Without *self-love,* Aristotle purported that a human was not able to extend sympathy and affection. Aristotle also didn't feel that self-love was hedonistic or egotistic. Aristotle felt self-love was a reflection of your pursuit of the noble, virtuous and self-reflective life—the life which leads you to **LIFE PLAN RIGHT**—becoming your highest potential.

Unfortunately, too many of us girls are raised to be highly critical about our looks—which creates the lack of self-love—the lack of self-esteem—and thereby the lack of the ability to become our **MIGHTIEST PRINCESS CHARMING SELF**—which lures in a Prince Charming.

Unfortunately this emphasis on looks starts very early on in a girl's life. There's a lot of societal pressure on young girls to be babes—even when they've barely outgrown being mere babies.

A recent report from Girls Inc. shared how far too many young girls have this need to be what they called "Super Girl" thin. Last year 60% of girls ages eight to twelve said that they believed to be popular, you must be thin—a rise up from 48% of girls in 2000. Sadly, as girls get older, their overall worries about appearance get worse.

In grades 3–5, 54% of girls worry about their appearance.

In grades 6–8, 74% of girls worry about their appearance.

In grades 9–12, 76% of girls worry about their appearance.

Also, according to The American Society for Aesthetic Plastic Surgery, in 1997 there were 59,890 procedures performed on patients under 18. Cut to the cosmetic cutting being performed in 2007—and there's a tremendous increase to 205,119 procedures performed on patients under 18! And obviously this **"APPEARANCE-CENTRISM"** doesn't stop at high school graduation. I know far too many women in their twenties and onward who never outgrew an extreme sense of beauty awareness. Sadly, a 2006 *Times Online* article citing a British magazine survey of 5,000 women had this report to share:

"The average woman worries about her body every 15 minutes, more frequently than men think about sex."

The least popular body parts: thighs (hated by 87%) and waists (disliked by 79%). Thankfully, one body part was found to be angst-free. No. Not the brain. Women found their ankles to be very lovable.

I am happy to simultaneously report that there are many men out there who aren't choosing love by the poundage. My friend David told me he fell in love with his wonderful wife of 13 years because he adored her "world lens"—for all the interesting perspectives she shared about life. David's idea of love (being turned on by how his paramour looked at the world—instead of by how she looked to the world) is a **RELATIONSHIP OF SHARED VIRTUE**. Hence, David is obviously a Prince Charming who fell in love with his Scheherazade.

Thankfully, there are many Prince Charmings like David out there hoping to find their Scheherazade— men who are not so obsessed with a woman looking perfect on the outside—but caring more about a woman being amazing on the inside—men who are not looking for "sex objects" to marry (and be eventually bored by)—men who are preferring to seek "happily ever after long-lasting, exciting, soul-nurturing love"!

MY GREATER WORLD HOPE:

Together we need to do something more as a society to change unrealistic expectations for female thinness and beauty. And to do so, we need to start early on by telling young girls (and young boys!) that a girl is amazing not because of what she looks like—but because of all the fabulous things she does and who she is! And while we're at it, I'd love to re-define **"TROPHY GIRL"** so it starts to mean "a girl who's amazing for all the fabulous things she does and who she is!"

With all that said . . . let me add the following very important caveat.

SELF-LOVE ALSO INCLUDES EATING HEALTHFULLY AND WORKING OUT AND DRESSING NICELY

*If you truly have self-love for yourself, you will want to eat foods that keep you operating at your **MIGHTIEST HUMAN BEING SELF** potential. This means you will eat the appropriate amount of calories each day to give you energy—without making you feel bloated and nauseous and like you need to take a nap. You will also get to the gym, and work out because you* *need good energy and a good mood to go out there and pillage and conquer your **UNIQUE SPECIFIC FUNCTION** and share your Schehrezade-fascinating tales in the most adorable way with your Prince Charming. Plus you need to feel sexy and sensual and happy in your body—because all of that is part of being your **MIGHTIEST HUMAN BEING SELF**—your Princess Charming Self. Aristotle was no prude. He was all about sensory pleasures of the body! So you must do what you can from your end—to love your body— even if in the end your "end" is not a perfectly toned and tiny "end." You must at least show your self-love by treating your body with self love! I repeat: You must feed your body well and take your body for walks—or out cycling—or whatever else you want to do to show your body your self-love for it!*

Basically, you want to attract a man who loves you for your whole *Princesss Charming Self*—because you want to attract a **RELATIONSHIP OF SHARED VIRTUE**. This means you must not simply rely on using *"a hot, perfectly toned body"* as your bait to lure in a man— or you will only be luring in a **RELATIONSHIP OF PLEASURE** or a **RELATIONSHIP OF UTILITY**. Instead, you must use *"Your Whole Enchilada Bait"* to lure in a man.

WHAT ARE THE INGREDIENTS FOR "YOUR WHOLE ENCHILADA BAIT"?

I. You must show self-love for your soul—by pursuing your passions and stimulating your soul with lots of growth.

II. Show self-love for your body—by treating your body well and loving it—imperfections and all.

III. If you're feeling insecure about your body, build up your self-esteem by working out more and eating a healthy diet. If you're doing everything in your *"high character"* control to be your *"highest potential body," you* will feel more confident and sexy!

IV. Every woman has at least one *"wildly sexy"* aspect: hair, eyes, boobs, butt, arms, back, legs, smile, fashion sense. Accentuate this positive, and nobody will notice your less-than-stellar aspects.

V. Forgive yourself for not being perfect by keeping in mind this fab story about Coco Chanel. When Coco accidentally singed her hair, instead of feeling insecure and unattractive about her new "hairdon't," she boldly chopped off her hair even more. Coco then proudly went to the opera with this short tomboyish hairstyle. Almost immediately she started a new fashion trend. The next day, women began visiting their hair salons, requesting Coco's hairstyle.

VI. Never complain about your "fatness" to a guy. You will only draw extra attention to your problematic areas—which makes no sense! Why lead a guy to notice something less than amazing about yourself, that he might not have noticed in the first place?

THE GOOD NEWS:

Everyone talks about looking for a relationship with someone with whom they share *"good chemistry"*—

not someone with *"perfect looks."* Basically, there is no such thing as *"perfect looks."* Some guys love big tooshes. Other guys love the waif look. One man's vanilla blond-haired babe—is another man's chocolate brunette-haired babe. Hence why attraction is more about *"good chemistry"*—because there is no such thing as a universally appealing *"perfect looks."*

So . . . what exactly is *"good chemistry"*? It's when you create the following *"bad math formula"*:

$$1 + 1 = 3$$

"Good chemistry" happens when you and your Prince Crush feel like together you add up to something more than you do apart.

When you're with the right guy you will feel extra good about yourself—from your crooked nose to your too big toes! You will be jiving together on so many levels that the details of your "large ears" or "those pesky 5 extra pounds" won't even begin to weigh down your love! You will even feel "safe" to occasionally gain a few pounds—without worrying he will judge you or dump you. When you're with the right guy, you will feel loved for your body and soul—for your WHOLE ENCHILADA SELF!

Oh—and just as you should love yourself with your bodily imperfections and all—you must learn to love your Prince Charming with his various imperfections—bodywise and otherwise! Coming up are helpful pointers to "troubleshoot" problems with your prince—without wanting to shoot your prince!

CHAPTER

8

Troubleshoot Relationship Problems With Your Prince

(Without Wanting To Shoot Your Prince)

Love at first sight is easy. It's love at 1,001st sight that can be very difficult. Actually, even love at 101st sight can even start to get a bit hairy—which I guess is about the same time that you allow your legs to get a bit hairy and walk around in front of your man without any makeup on. This is also simultaneously a time that coincides with when your man begins to fart in bed and walk around without his metaphysical make up on. Meaning? It's a time your man starts to reveal his nonsocialized nonperfect face to you.

GUESS WHAT ELSE? This is also an exciting time lovewise—because it's when true love really blooms for you and your man. It's a time when both of you stop trying to be 100% perfect—and begin to finally show your true *superinsideyourself selves*.

THE PROBLEM? You and your partner are not always *"super"* inside your *superinsideyourself selves*. Humans are human after all —as Aristotle recognized in many of his philosophical passages, including this ditty of his here:

"If a man is a man because he resembles an ideal man, there must still be a more ideal man to whom both ordinary men and the ideal men are similar."

Scholars have had many conflicting interpretations of the exact meaning of this ditty—but the analysis I'm going with is this one:

There Is No Such Thing
As An "Ideal" Man.
Nobody's Perfect.

Everyone of us has a little streak of asshole in us— hopefully only a slight wedgie of a streak of asshole. But the point is—there is a big danger in having expectations for a fantasy ideal partner. Sure it's good to have a concept of an ideal partner—but the real ideal partner is someone who is as close as possible to being ideal—within rational reason.

True love is what happens when disappointment sets in and disagreements unfold. Eventually the going is gonna get rough—and when it does, it's up to both you and your man to speak up with high character integrity—and not act out.

As I mentioned earlier, John Gottman, founder of The Love Lab, says a relationship will survive *not* based on how well you get along, but by how well you *don't* get along. A couple is only as strong as how well the two can deal with their weakest moments.

Voila . . . Gottman's 3 Strategies For Dealing With Conflict:

I. avoidance/stonewalling (the worst)

II. fighting (better than avoidance, but still not health-ful or helpful)

III. validation (the winning method—which means really trying to see things from the other person's point of view, and sharing all views with kindness, and the goal of finding a win-win compromise!)

Gottman puts forth that avoidance/stonewalling is the numero uno contributor to the finito of love because it says to your partner:

"Yo! I've checked out of this discussion because I don't find you important enough to continue to talk to anymore."

Ouch. Basically, stonewalling conveys a lack of respect. Interestingly, studies show that most men are physiologically unaffected by their wives' stonewalling. However, stonewalling has quite the opposite affect on women. Wives' heart rates increase dramatically when their husbands stonewall. To add to this, about 85% of stonewallers are men! Admittedly, handling the inevitable stresses of a relationship is not an easy task.

Voila . . . Aristotle's View On Conflict:

"Anybody can become angry—that is easy, but to be angry with the right person and to the right degree and at the right time and for the right purpose, and in the right way—that is not within everybody's power and is not easy."

TRANSLATION? When problems arise, it takes **THE VIRTUE OF DISCIPLINE** to resist lapsing into avoidance/stonewalling or outright fighting. It takes **THE VIRTUE OF DISCIPLINE** to self-examine with **CONSCIOUS INSIGHT** to assess your self-responsibility within a problem. It takes **THE VIRTUE OF DISCIPLINE** to do the right thing and to be a good person when the going gets rough. For the most part, human beings aren't bad. Human beings are simply weak. Human beings simply just don't want to put in **THE VIRTUE OF DISCIPLINE** to be good and behave with high integrity.

Believe me, I know how hard it is to be good during bad times. Unfortunately, being a good person isn't just something that happens naturally—like growing taller or hairier. However, being good, kind, considerate, empathetic, self-responsible—all these high-integrity values—is worth the **VIRTUE OF DISCIPLINE**—because every low-integrity, immoral action sways you—swerves you farther—then further—away from your most important aim: soul-nurture your way to happiness—towards **LIFE PLAN RIGHT**. As Aristotle said:

"Virtue is a character concerned with choice."

And it's always your choice:

I. You can behave cold, hurtful, stonewalling in the immediate gratification moment—and cash in on the low-level pleasure this brings!

*II. You can tap into the virtue of **DISCIPLINE** and speak up warmly, because you recognize soul-nurturing love is a human's main source for true happiness—not the satisfaction of being right in the moment!*

TO SUM IT UP:

If you want to live happily ever after with your Prince Charming, it is absolutely essential you put in the virtue of **DISCIPLINE**. Hence why two of the top 5 essential traits for true love are:

I. You and your partner must want to grow.

*II. You and your partner must understand that a relationship is not simply a **DEN OF PLEASURE**. It is also a **LABORATORY FOR GROWTH**—a place where you learn to harness the virtue of **DISCIPLINE** to become **YOUR MIGHTIEST HUMAN BEING SELF**.*

SOME GOOD NEWS ABOUT BEING GOOD:

People become happier by doing good actions and unhappier by doing bad actions. The more bad actions you do—the easier it becomes to do bad actions. However the more good actions you do—the easier it becomes to do good actions—and so you will tend to do more of them over time.

Aristotle said it well when he said:

"You become just by performing just actions, temperate by performing temperate actions, brave by performing brave actions."'

Aristotle could also have added:

*"You eventually become a jerk by behaving like a jerk. Because every time you behave like a jerk, you veer a little left from **LIFE PLAN RIGHT** and start heading towards **LIFE PLAN WRONG**."*

Basically, you want to make sure you're doing as many *just actions, temperate actions, and brave actions* as you can—as often as possible—so you keep on wanting to do them. With this in mind, I want to give you some helpful relationship troubleshooting techniques for performing *just actions, temperate actions* and *brave actions*— instead of *jerk actions*.

Troubleshooting Techniques For Not Being A Jerk During Conflict:

I. Pick the right time, the right place. Do you have at least 30 minutes of uninterrupted time ahead? Are you in a place where you can talk openly and not self-

consciously? In general, the best place to talk is alone in your home, where you can sit facing each other, with good strong eye contact.

II. Avoid harsh start-ups. According to Gottman, he can predict 96% of the time how a conversation will end based on its first three minutes. Use the virtue of DISCIPLINE and CONSCIOUS INSIGHT to avoid using criticism, sarcasm or cruel words. Don't start out blaming—or calling your partner bad names—or your partner will spend more time defending himself than attending to your needs and feelings. Instead, try beginning with a compliment about what you appreciate about your partner. Also, include a reminder about how you really want to work on your relationship so it succeeds and you both can grow together. Begin by calmly explaining how the conflict affects you—your feelings, values, dreams, goals. Recognize that eventually most fights do not stay about the fight's topic—but rather the "way" people choose to fight—and consciously choose to share your concerns with warmth and integrity.

III. Don't try to convince your partner you are right. Instead of trying to win arguments, try to have a winning relationship! How? Try talking in "I" sentences instead of "you" sentences—so you speak more about how you feel. (And "I think you are a jerk!" is not an example of an "I" statement!) Your goal is to get your partner to empathize—so forget about harping on details and facts. Keep staying with your feelings, values, dreams, goals. From this place of empathy, your partner will better hear you—and thereby want to find a way to take care of your needs and feelings. If the conversation escalates, be sure to tell your partner that you recognize that your point of view is relative. Your truth is not necessarily the whole truth and nothing but the truth. Be ready to be convinced out of your anger and misery. As Stephen Covey brilliantly stated in his fabulous book The Seven Habits of Highly Effective People: *"Seek first to understand—then to be understood!"*

*IV. Put in the virtue of **DISCIPLINE** to calm yourself before you begin talking. Although studies show that yelling is better than stonewalling, yelling has its share of problems. Studies show when people yell, they get themselves even angrier. Interesting factoid: If you and/or your partner's heartbeat becomes higher than 100 beats per minute during an argument, you will not be able to fully understand/process what the other is saying. Basically, when you're angry, your brain's processing becomes blocked, and it's literally more difficult to solve problems and express yourself clearly. Plus—duh—you're more likely to foolishly inflame the situation with insults and petty meannesses. As Marcus Aurelius said: "How much more grievous are the consequences of anger, than the causes of it."*

V. If you are upset at your partner for something specific that they did, try not to generalize their action by saying, "You always do this. You always say that." Generalizations will only escalate your partner's emotional state because they're more vague to discuss, and less believable. Come on. Be honest with yourself. A realistic "always" action is a very rare thing. Psychologists all agree it's best to limit your talk to the one specific recent event that is bugging you, and make past offenses not admissible evidence.

*VI. I said it before—and I'll keep saying it: I believe nearly all our lessons in life are lessons in learning how to get better at loving and being loved. If your partner is angry with you, recognize that his anger is a misdirected plea for love. Your partner's simply upset because he feels something you said or did was a sign of not loving him enough. View his anger through this lens. When you have this **CONSCIOUS INSIGHT** about anger, you can more swiftly feel better about sharing loving words and a loving response with your angry partner.*

VII. If you're upset with your partner, name the exact emotions you are feeling. For example: angry, resentful, hurt, embarrassed, humiliated, vulnerable, afraid, uptight, depressed. Researcher Matthew Lieberman from UCLA discovered that simply straightforwardly recognizing that you're feeling a negative emotion—like anger—can calm this emotion by 50%—because it halves your "amygdala activation" to consciously observe your emotions. I want you to double up the benefits of this halving. After you've named a negative emotion, rename it with a positive. Consciously decide to replace each negative emotion with one of the following words: acceptance, forgiveness, surrendering, empathy, warmth, love, understanding. Contemplate this word, over and over, as if it were a mantra.

VIII. Music has been said to soothe the savage beast. I've witnessed for myself how turning up the volume *on my ipod can turn down the angry thoughts in my head. Neuroscientists say music taps into the same pleasure centers in the brain as orgasms. Aristotle was also a big fan of the cathartic powers of music. He prescribed music as a medical cure—saying it helped to "purge an excess of emotion." To quote my philosopher buddy: "When [people] have made use of the melodies which fill the soul with orgiastic feeling, they are brought back by these sacred melodies to a normal condition as if they had been medically treated and undergone a purge [**CATHARSIS**]." If you're angry at your partner, you can get yourself to sing a new, happier tune, by singing along with your favorite tunes. One recent study by The Institute of Music, Health and Education found that even a mere 5 minutes of singing can put you in a more positive mood.*

__IX.__ If interruptions are invading an angry discussion, slow down and segment up. Decide to give each of yourselves your own segmented 10 minute expression non-interruptus time block to talk and be heard— until you both feel heard.

__X.__ Make sure your body language is not cursing and shouting. It's very harmful to a conversation with your sweetie if your arms are crossed or your face is sneering. Studies show it helps to hold each other's hands while having a difficult conversation because due to Neural Linguistic Programming it taps into the "I love you" reminders in your brain.

__XI.__ Close a difficult conversation by purposefully sharing memories of good times you've shared and *good qualities you love about your partner, so as to jumpstart loving memories, and defuse bad ones. If it's been a while since you've felt that lusty, feisty feeling of romance, you can jump start this phase anew, by going back to those first few romantic courtship places. Chances are you will re-feel the love thanks to the romance feng shui of this place—and you will experience deja romance all over again. Also be sure to end a difficult conversation by creating an obvious upside to talking—so you and your partner will want to share honest difficult conversations again. In other words, be sure to close the conversation by consciously listing all the positive things you learned thanks to the perk of the virtue of **DISCIPLINE**.*

*__XII.__ Stay conscious of maintaining what Gottman calls "a 5 to 1 ratio of nice to nasty moments." Gottman discovered that couples who remain married versus divorced often experienced just as much conflict— but put in more "repair." They were nicer to each other with a ratio of 5 nice moments to 1 tornado moment. If you're having problems with your honey, add a little more honey to that love ointment! Toss a compliment. Send a silly e-mail. Plan a fun night out—or an even funner night in. Cuddle more. Spoon more. Spork more. Not only will your partner feel more loving to you, but you will feel more loving to your partner—thanks to a little something called **"COGNITIVE DISSONANCE"**— which can be summed up like this: We humans don't like to have a disparity between our actions and our beliefs/feelings. When we change our actions to loving actions, we change our beliefs/feelings to loving beliefs/feelings. For example, if Human A does a loving action for Human B—through **COGNITIVE***

*DISSONANCE—Human A's brain will tell them, "Geez, I must surely love Human B if I'm doing a loving action for them!" Human A will then wind up loving Human B a wee bit more. Meaning? Even if you and your partner are upset at one another, if you both tap into the virtue of **DISCIPLINE**, and behave lovingly to one another—eventually you will jumpstart loving feelings once again.*

***XIII.** If you've been feeling especially tense with your partner, show yourself some self-loving. Are you eating right? Are you sleeping enough? Are you exercising regularly? Are you extra-stressed from work? If you're going through a particularly stressful time, load up on B Vitamins, calcium and magnesium. Plus, be sure to supplement your SAM-e levels—which is a naturally occurring molecule produced in the body that becomes depleted due to stress, age and diet. Terrific poducts like Nature Made SAM-e Complete replenish the body's natural SAM-e levels in as few as 7 to 14 days when taken on a daily basis. (To find out if SAM-e Complete is right for you, go to www. sam-e.com) I am also a big believer in the power of meditation to help create a happier brain. Meditation is not just a Buddhist mumbo-jumbo suggestion. It's been neuroscientifically shown to improve the flow of your neural pathways and calm your mood.*

If you practice the above troubleshooting tips regularly, you will be giving yourself a form of *Love Insurance*—by guarding your love from getting over-heated and thereby breaking down.

The Question However Does Remain:

What if you and your man keep having repeated problems and conflicts? How do you know if you're merely experiencing temporary speed bumps as you head on down the path towards living happily ever love—versus—how do you know if you should dump the chump?

Margaret Atwood had a wonderfully impactful metaphor in one of her books that relates to this question. She described how you could boil to death in a bathtub if someone just slowly turns up the heat on the water—and thereby you don't notice that the water is reaching boiling zone.

Far too often a Prince Crush starts out very nice, then slowly turns up the heat on his naughtiness. Indeed, this is exactly what occurred with my Prince Harming—who did a "date and switch" from being lovingly wonderful to being my cheating-don't-get-me-started Teacher.

If you keep asking your friends: "Is this normal?"— guess what? Chances are your Prince Crush's behaviors are not normal—and your man is entering into the Prince Harming Zone!

A BASIC LIFE PRINCIPLE:

If you need to ask, then chances are you already know!

Unfortunately many women give their Prince Crushes far too much leeway for their bad behavior—because they believe in the following quote by Desiderius Erasmus:

"In the land of the blind, the one-eyed man is king."

MEANING? After a few bad dating experiences, many women start to get cynical about the lack of quality men available. As a result, many women feel that most of the men out there are the **"METAPHOR-ICAL QUALITY EQUIVALENT"** of being "completely blind." So if one of these cynical sorts of women meets a guy who has at least the **"METAPHORICAL QUALITY EQUIVALENT"** of one good eye (or even one bad eye), then this cynical sort of woman believes that this is as good as a guy gets, so it's good enough!

I SAY: I don't want you to dare become one of these cynical sorts of women!

I SAY: If you lower your dating bar too low, then all that will come slithering to you will be low-life wormy guys. You must raise that bar—raise your expecta-tions—and you will raise your awareness of where to find and how to snag a true Prince Charming!

I SAY: Don't waste precious time-ticking-time with the wrong partner! It's better to have a short bad relationship than a long bad relationship!

I SAY: Wake up, oh sleeping beauty, and find out if you should make up or break up—via the helpful conscious insight tips in Chapter 9!

CHAPTER

9

Wake Up, Oh Sleeping Beauty!

(How To Know If You Should Break Up Or Make Up)

Before I met my Prince Charming, I used to joke that if there were indeed life on another planet, there was a quick way we humans could assess if these aliens were a more advanced life-form. And no, we humans did not need to ask these aliens to check out their technology—to see if they had iPhones and Facebook. We simply needed to ask the aliens if they had dating. If the aliens did not have dating, it was indeed proof they were a far more evolved species. Basically, dating can be painful, confusing, daunting.

OR TO WORD IT BLUNTLY: DATING CAN TRULY SUCK.

Back in my dating days B. M. P.C. (before my Prince Charming) I used to joke that all dating should be renamed *"blind dating"*—and instead of saying I'm "seeing someone," I should be more honest and say *"I'm dimly viewing someone."*

Thankfully, it's now fully clear to me why I couldn't see men clearly. My lack of 20/20 vision for viewing men came from my lack of 20/20 insight. I wasn't tapping into my *blessed* **CONSCIOUS INSIGHT**—and looking to see what a man was bringing to both the long-term table and short-term bedside.

IN OTHER WORDS:

I wasn't keeping my eye on the long-term happily ever after prize of finding a **RELATIONSHIP OF SHARED VIRTUE!**

Instead I was foolishly being lured into **RELATIONSHIPS OF PLEASURE** and **RELATIONSHIPS OF UTILITY**—never understanding the important distinction between seeking *superinsideoneself* happiness with a man—versus merely settling for *superficial pleasure* with a man! As a result . . .

I. Sometimes I'd stay with a Prince Harming for far too long—because I was hypnotized by his *superficial lures* (sexiness, wealthiness, funniness, etc.).

II. Sometimes I'd break up with a damn fabulous Prince Charming for the silliest superficial reasons—or over the silliest fights—because I was not willing to put in the **VIRTUES OF COURAGE AND DISCIPLINE** to make love a **LABORATORY FOR MY GROWTH**.

In this chapter I want to help you to see with 20/20 **CONSCIOUS INSIGHT** who a man is—and who you are being—because you need to view both *your man* rightly and *yourself* rightly for you to know for sure if you should break up or make up.

IT'S LIKE THIS:

Whenever you want to break up with a man, it's usually because of one of 4 reasons!

4 Reasons to Break Up

I. *Your man* is not your soul mate—he doesn't "get" you in your soul—and motivate you to grow into your highest potential—therefore you're not aimed towards **LIFE PLAN RIGHT.**

II. *Your man* is not ready to grow into his highest potential—therefore you're not aimed toward **LIFE PLAN RIGHT.**

III. *You (yes, you!)* are not ready to grow into your highest potential—therefore you're not aimed toward **LIFE PLAN RIGHT.**

IV. *You (yes, you!)* have unrealistic expectations for love—and what exactly it means to be aimed toward **LIFE PLAN RIGHT.**

Let's first look at troublesome reason **#III** for a breakup—where you're the responsible guilty reason for the buh-bye factor. It's funny how we all think it is a laughing matter to say at break up time:

"It's not you, it's me."

Although this famous breakup line has always been considered a supposed joke, it is indeed often truly the reason for many a love affair ending. All too often it is our very own self who is getting in our own way of true love and happiness.

A BIG SECRET FOR LONG-LASTING TRUE LOVE:

When problems arise in a relationship, you must not only use your fabulous lens of **20/20 CONSCIOUS INSIGHT** to look at the character problems and growth issue problems of your man—but to look at who you are being—your own damn character issues and your own damn growth issues!

Basically, too many people look at their partner through a *magnifying glass,* and don't bother to look at themselves in the *mirror!*

BE FOREWARNED!

If you break up with a man without fully looking at yourself in the mirror, you could be on your way to duplicating your love problems—a la Groundhog Day—over and over.

Yo! Keep in mind! Wherever you go, there your pesky repeated issues are!

For this reason, before you break up with a man, I strongly recommend you take the time to ask yourself if there's something you're doing to create (and re-create) conflict! Is there something you must put in the **VIRTUES OF COURAGE AND DISCIPLINE** to change about yourself!

Here's some helpful prompters to allow you to see yourself more clearly in the mirror with *greater* **20/20 CONSCIOUS INSIGHT.**

Mirror, Mirror, Off The Wall: Thinking and Feeling Habits For Better Inner-Self Knowledge

I. Be honest with yourself! Do you have the same patterns of problems you keep dragging into every relationship? Remember: You are the common denominator in all your relationship problems! **MEANING?** If you break up with this man, you might just be dragging those same issues—your same emotional baggage—into your next relationship—so you experience déjà angst all over again! Hence it's important you set aside some time to talk with your man about each of your childhoods—the good, bad, and dysfunctional. Recognize: Usually there's a **REPETITION COMPULSION/PORTABLE CHILDHOOD SCENARIO** at the root of both of your ongoing conflicts with one another. Psychologists Morrie and Arleah Shechtman, authors of a wonderful book called *Love In The Present Tense*, put forth a belief that if a fight lasts more than two minutes—and escalates into something god awful—then there's a childhood issue at its painful root. Discuss this with your man. Also, share the following conversation about a universal psychological belief about attraction: We subconsciously are attracted to someone who represents the best/worst of our parents, so we can try to re-create—then mend—our childhood disappointments about love. For this very reason, it's essential that before you break up with your partner, that you and your partner both talk about the best/worst qualities of your parents. Get vulnerable about your childhoods. You should both mutually agree to shed powerful **CONSCIOUS INSIGHT** light on the darker zones of your past, in the hopes of revealing—then healing—your past pain—so you don't get into repeated patterns of pain—à la **REPETITION COMPULSION/PORTABLE CHILDHOOD SCENARIOS.**

II. Are you—without knowing it—an annoyingly irksome person? Find out by asking for an **"EQUAL SHARE TIME"** about your annoyingly irksome habits. Trade telling one another what you find annoyingly irksome about one another. Swap **"SAME VALUE HABIT COMPLAINTS"** like **"SAME VALUE BASEBALL CARDS."** Start with a teeny annoyingly irksome habit complaint each of you can tell each of you. Afterwards, build up to a huge complaint. The reason why it's good to swap: You both must empathize with how it feels to be told you're annoyingly irksome. Plus you both must feel an equal sense of "growth opportunity"— feeling like you both have issues you need to work on for the sake of almighty happily ever after love. William Faulkner said: *"If I were to choose between pain and nothing, I would choose pain."* **MEANING?** Choose the temporary pain of finding out how you're each annoyingly irksome, so you can avoid breaking up and being left with nothing.

III. Is there something you're hurt about—or worried about—that you have yet to tell your man—and so it's hurting your love because you expect your man to be a mind reader? Hate to break it to you, but even mind readers are not really mind readers! They're clever showbiz folks. **MEANING?** If a mind reader is not truly a mind reader, neither is your partner! Speak up! If something is on your mind ... share it! One of my favorite quotes is from Emile Zola: *"I came into this world to live out loud."* Live out loud, dammit! Your love life is only as strong as your open communication!

IV. Is your partner getting on your nerves because your relationship is suffering from "static clinging"? Do you take enough breaks—give each other enough space? The best relationship is one that does not foster too much independence—nor too much dependence—but exists in that healthy moderation **"MEAN ZONE"** of *interdependence.* Take a step back and look to see if you and your man need to take more steps away.

V. Are there *"never, ever, ever going to give up for the sake of love"* deal breakers which you're just realizing you have now? If so, maybe you're having a *"silent fight"* with your partner about these deal breakers. Maybe your man is willing to be a *"deal bender"* on these issues. If you don't talk about your fears about your deal breakers, you could turn into a *"Negative Evidence Collector"*—and start looking for evidence of him being wrong for you which is not really there— you're just doing it to protect yourself because you're afraid of this deal breaker busting up your love! So stop having a *"silent fight"* with your partner—and have an open, warm discussion instead!

VI. Are you sweating the small stuff—and thereby harming your relationship? Even though I am telling you to talk openly with your partner, you must do this within a moderation **"MEAN ZONE."** You must not nag and complain too much—or you will damage your relationship. Be honest with yourself! Can you learn to "bend" and not "break" on certain issues you complain about? Set the following intention: *"I will not complain about anything to my partner for the next 3 days."* Would this be an incredibly hard intention for you to fulfill? If so, maybe you're looking at your partner through an incredibly negative lens because you're overworked and under-exercised. Take a good exercise class ASAP! I recommend Exhale's Core Fusion classes—because they offer a holistic approach to exercise—detoxing and toning you in mind, body and spirit.

VII. Are you revealing to your partner your *superinsideyou self?* This means sharing the teeniest of your day's details along with your biggest of dreams. Psychologist Dr. Jani offers up a fascinating theory on successful bonding—called *"the sound relationship house theory"*—which is basically about the importance of two people being able to appreciate ordinary everyday moments together. These shared ordinary moments, Dr. Jani found, were the key not only to successful marital relationships—but friendships. And these shared ordinary moments were also what created a better sex life for couples! In fact, according to studies, talking about daily details with your partner is just as important as sharing big-time hopes and fears. If you're not feeling close to your partner, it could be because you're not allowing yourself to get close by openly sharing the big and small stuff in your life. Psychologists recommend you start your day by asking each other: *"Anything special going on today?"* At the end of the day, ask, *"Hey, how did that special something go today?"* Also at end of day ask: *"What made you happy today? What were you most proud of today? What were you surprised about today?"*

VIII. Leo Buscaglia has said: *"A great deterrent to love is found in anyone who fears change, for ... growing, learning, experiencing is change. Change is inevitable."* Be honest with yourself! Are you only viewing your relationship as a **"DEN OF PLEASURE"** for fun and companionship—and not recognizing that you must put in *the virtues of* **COURAGE** *and* **DISCIPLINE** to grow into your **MIGHTIEST HUMAN BEING SELF**— so you can grow your love to its mightiest potential?

IX. As we women all know, we women love shoes! So here's an opportunity to get more shoes as you get more love! Sounds pretty fabulous, huh? Ready? You must learn to put yourself in your partner's shoes more often—so you will more successfully understand how your partner feels—and thereby feel more love for your partner—instead of just feeling like he's a big creepy jerk you need to break up with! This opinion is shared both by Stephen Covey who said, *"Seek first to understand, then to be understood!"* and Aristotle who wrote about something called **"MIMESIS"**— which is all about how we humans can learn more about ourselves and others through mirroring one another. Interestingly, many modern therapists—from bigwigs like Freud and onward—advocate Aristotle's belief in the powers of **"MIMESIS"**—instructing patients in therapy to "play act"—swap their role in a problem from participant to observer. Basically, we humans love mimicry. As babies we learn from mimicry—imitating what we see and hear. Later, as adults, we get a big kick out of anything that reminds us of us—like monkeys in a zoo—or how dolphins can sort of speak. We're built to appreciate mimicry – and built to learn from mimicry. **MEANING?** When you consciously "play act" a relationship problem from your man's point of view (using **"MIMESIS"**) you are built to learn how to see yourself and your relationship problems much better. You're hard wired to learn more via **"MIMESIS"**—to tap into **CONSCIOUS INSIGHT** better. So before you think those boots are made for walking out of your present relationship, try on your man's shoes—and consciously view your relationship from his point of view instead!

X. Do you handle conflict in a less than stellar manner? Do you stonewall? Do you rant and rave? Are you being a Princess Harming or a Princess Charming when you express yourself during conflict? Are you the troublemaking instigator of most of your conflicts in the first place? Once again, if you want a lasting (and lusting) relationship you must be charming not only during the good times, but the bad times. You must deal with conflict using the *virtue of* **DISCIPLINE**—and really choose to be loving during these challenging times when you're tempted to not be your most loving self. You must ask yourself: *"How would love deal with this issue?*

What would love do?" You must tell yourself: *"It's more important to be loving than to be right!"*

Okay. Enough about you, you, you! Let's take a good 20/20 **CONSCIOUS INSIGHT** look at your Prince Crush—and find out if you should be loving him or leaving him!

If you picked your Prince Crush simply because he was only a superficial infatuation, then you're wanting to leave him right now is the right choice. Basically, if you picked your Prince Crush using a myopic short-term lens—you might now be experiencing this urge to leave him because you've wisely shifted focus to your long-term lens—and are now wisely seeing your Prince Crush doesn't satisfy those essential 5 out of 5 traits!

If this is the case, you are not alone in selecting your partner with a short-term immediate gratification lens. Most people view selecting a partner (and a career!) with a short-term lens. Most people do not bother to put in *the virtue of* **DISCIPLINE** to take the time to view a love opportunity (or a career opportunity!) with that necessary long-term lens focused on your long-term end goal for life. If this is indeed why you want to break up, I support you in having the virtue of **COURAGE** and **DISCIPLINE** to break up with your man—since you're now realizing he's a Prince Harming not a Prince Charming. Hey, it's better to have a short bad relationship than a long bad relationship.

And don't you dare beat yourself up about your bad choice. Learn from it—and decide to from here on in always keep those 5 essential traits in mind when Prince Charming Shopping.

However, with that said, there's also a secondary reason for wanting to break up with a man after the hot steamy smoke of the Infatuation Phase dissipates:

You have unrealistic expectations for love!

I want you to be able to fully differentiate between these two reasons, before you break up with your man. Hence, it's important that you take the time now to view your Prince Crush through a long-term lens—so you can suss out *for sure* if you're wanting to break up with him is because:

I. Your Prince Crush won't lead you to a happily ever after **LIFE PLAN RIGHT** future.

II. You have unrealistic expectations of what a happily ever after **LIFE PLAN RIGHT** future is really all about!

LISTEN UP!

You must accept something right here—right now—that the delicious, blissful honeymoon period of infatuation you felt for your man when you first met him will never be able to be sustained 100% full force in that euphoric state—and that's okay—even expected!

"Flagging passions are not necessarily a red flag to leave a relationship," says clinical psychologist Barry McCarthy. *"You must accept: It's difficult—if not near impossible—for the early days of passion and romance to sustain themselves."*

TRANSLATION: If you want to be part of a perfect couple, you must accept you will be part of an "imperfect couple." You will have ebbs in all your fun-filled flow. You will not always feel 100% in love with your partner 100% of the time. And that's okay—as long as you both keep your eyes on the long-term prize—your long-term teleology—of wanting to grow into your **MIGHTIEST HUMAN BEING SELVES.**

YOU MUST ALWAYS REMEMBER:

A relationship serves two functions! It's both a **DEN OF PLEASURE** and a **LABORATORY FOR GROWTH!** You cannot hang out in the den all the time. Occasionally you have to wander into that laboratory!

If you want a second doctor's opinion on the ebbs and flows of love, just ask the famed Dr. Gottman—founder of The Love Lab—who has discovered that long-term, happily married couples disagree just as much as couples who divorce. The only difference? Happily married couples accept there will be disagreements. Happily married couples value growing and working through their problems—for the sake of being in long-term, supportive, growing coupledom. Happily married couples recognize that relationships serve that double function of **DEN OF PLEASURE** *and* **LABORATORY FOR GROWTH!**

Lucky you! You are a human and so you have the perk of **CONSCIOUS INSIGHT TO** help you figure out if you want to break up with your man because:

I. Your Prince Crush won't lead you to a happily ever after **LIFE PLAN RIGHT** future.

II. You have unrealistic expectations of what a happily ever after **LIFE PLAN RIGHT** future is really all about!

Ready to view your Prince Crush with a high-powered light of **CONSCIOUS INSIGHT?** First, calm your mind. Become aware of your breath. Breathe out fear. Breathe in love. Now look at those 5 essential traits for a Prince Charming and ask yourself if you honestly feel your Prince Crush is offering up these 5 traits:

Prince Charming Trait #1: Does he want to be in a committed relationship? (Basically, does he embrace character values that match with your values for a committed happily ever after future? Are there "value deal breakers" when it comes to marriage, monogamy, kids, religion, etc?)

Prince Charming Trait #2: Does he value growing as a person? (Basically, does he embrace character values that show he has an open and growing soul—values wanting to become his highest potential—owning self-responsibility and seeking insights?)

Prince Charming Trait #3: Does he understand that a relationship serves 2 functions. It's not solely a **"DEN OF PLEASURE"**—*it's also a soul's* **"LABORATORY FOR GROWTH"** *(Basically, does he embrace character values which show he absolutely wants a* **"RELATIONSHIP OF SHARED VIRTUE"***?)*

Prince Charming Trait #4: Does he make you feel "safe" enough in the relationship to allow you to reach your fullest potential? (Surprise: The top feeling a relationship should inspire is "safety." Without safety, you will never arrive at feeling love—because you won't allow yourself to be vulnerable enough for true intimacy. If your man embraces high-integrity character values, then you will trust him enough to reveal your truest self!)

Prince Charming Trait #5: Is your man happy? (Surprise: If you want to live happily ever after, your man has to be happy! If he's unhappy all the time, he will view you through non-rosy, dark-lensed life glasses! You need to find a man who embraces character values which help him be emotionally stable, even-tempered, addiction-free and full of high self esteem.)

I want you to shut up and meditate on these 5 essential traits—really ponder if your Prince Crush lives up to them all! Sometimes it's obvious you need to break up—because the pain you're feeling is so very great. Other times it's not so obvious, so here are some empowering **CONSCIOUS INSIGHT** prompters to allow you to better know if you want to break up with your man for **LIFE PLAN RIGHT REASONS** . . . or **LIFE PLAN WRONG REASONS!**

1. Do You Love Your Man Because He Has A Heart Of Gold—Or Comes with A Big Pot Of Gold?

Are you starting to lose your attraction to your man because you feel he's not rich and high-powered enough? If so, keep in mind that although the total absence of an income might bring its share of stress into a relationship, adamantly seeking a marital partner who's a millionaire won't necessarily guarantee you a lifetime of bliss. Consistently, studies show that individuals who prioritize wealth over close human connection tend to be less happy—and this is consistent in every culture.

Sociological researcher H. W. Perkins surveyed 800 college alumni, and discovered that those who reported "yuppie values" (preferring high income, job success and status over enjoying truly close friendships and highly-connected love relationships) were twice as likely to describe themselves as "fairly" or "very" unhappy. Interestingly, a similar correlation appeared among 7,167 college students surveyed in 41 countries. Those who prioritized love over money reported higher life satisfaction than their money-obsessed pals.

And what about that rumor:

Money problems are a top cause of divorce?

Mere hearsay—according to Jan Andersen, associate professor at CSU Sacramento, who did extensive sociological research and wrote a doctoral dissertation on this very subject. Andersen says:

"As a predictor of divorce, money problems are . . . so minor . . . If we look at all the causes of divorce, financial problems can only account for 5% of the effect."

On an interesting note, when Andersen first embarked on his research, his goal was to prove a cause/effect link between money/divorce. Andersen was both a child of divorce and a teacher of personal finance and so he liked the concept that improving money-managing skills might improve marriage success rates. However, to Andersen's surprise, the only research he found showing an actual link between money and divorce was merely one survey from 1948—of postwar divorced women who were asked what ended their marriages.

THEIR LEADING RESPONSE: "non-support."

TRANSLATION: Hubby wasn't providing enough money.

Andersen clarified that *"non-support"* was one of the only grounds you could use to get a divorce back then. Plus, this survey focused only on wives' opinions—not husbands. Recent research, however, has consistently shown money playing a far lesser role in divorce—usually ranking about fifth in the blame line-up behind incompatibility, lack of emotional support, abuse and sexual problems.

ANDERSEN'S HYPOTHESIS: Money is a more socially acceptable reason for divorce than confessing to abuse or sexual problems, so people claim it out loud more often.

ANOTHER ESSENTIAL POINT TO KEEP IN MIND:

Even when couples fight about money, they're often really fighting about more important underlying problems—claims Olivia Mellan, a Washington, D.C., therapist and author of *Money Harmony: Resolving Money Conflicts in Your Life and Relationships.* *"It's always what the money represents: dependency, control, freedom, security, pleasure, self-worth,"* explains Mellan.

THE LESSON TO BE LEARNED:

All the money in the world won't make you happy. But a loving highly-connected relationship will!

2. Do You Know The Difference Between Mind-Blowing Sex With Your Man—and Heart-Blowing Sex With Your Man?

Sex, sex, sex, sex, sex, sex, sex, sex, sex, sex, sex, sex. Everyone is always talking about sex. But is everyone always having sex? The answer is a resounding: nope. Even the most passionate couple might only have sex a few hours a day in the very beginning. Then later a few hours every few days. It's startling to reflect on how little time men and women truly spend indulging in sex in the grand scheme of a 24 hours a day, seven days a week life. Yet we all place such incredible value seeking a hot sex life with a partner.

MY BELIEF?

a. Having a hot sex life with your partner is highly important for staying connected soul-to-soul. You need to make sure your relationship stays a "**DEN OF PLEASURE**"—so your soul stays excited and stimulated with passion. With this in mind, you and your partner need to remain adventurous and curious to share ongoing new ways to indulge in sex. You need to feel "safe" to talk about your kinkiest of fantasies—and open-minded about indulging in one another's kinkiest of fantasies. You need to "grow" yourself sexually with your partner—challenge yourself sexually with your partner—so you don't get bored sexually. *Your* **DEN OF PLEASURE** *should double up as* **LABORATORY FOR SEXUAL GROWTH!**

b. Simultaneously, you need to *stop focusing sooo much on having a hot sex life—and refocus on having a* **HOT SENSUAL LIFE**. After all, your sensual life is a much bigger part of your every daily life! Your sensual life can be indulged in every second of the day. What do I mean by a **HOT SENSUAL LIFE?** It's all about loving your partner's way of cuddling, kissing, touching, caressing. Unlike with hot sex, you can indulge in a **HOT SENSUAL LIFE** for more than a mere hour a day—and you should! **MEANING?** Even on those days (and nights) (and early mornings) that you're not having hot sex, you can still feel hot sensual heat with your partner—by sitting next to each other in restaurants, holding hands as you walk down the street, going to bed at the same time so you can fall asleep holding each other, whispering sweet words of appreciation into each other's ears. The better you maintain your **HOT SENSUAL LIFE**, the better you maintain your hot sex life—and the more you will have heart-blowing sex—which is far more important than mind-blowing sex! After all, sex is in many ways just a dyslexic search for love! If you feel connected on a sensual level with your partner, chances are your sex life will be more exciting. And even if you don't have those mind-blowing orgasms, you will share amazing heart-blowing enchanting passion! Basically, it's more important to love the way your partner smells and feels every day—than it is to have climaxes every day!

3. Do You Love Your Partner For How He Superficially Looks To The World—Or For His *Superinsidehim* World Lens?

Read this Buddhist story, then meditate using your "horse sense" on if you've found your Prince Charming:

Once upon a time there was a King Horse Maven who loved collecting winning speedy race horses. To help gather his speedy horse collection, he hired a Super Talented Horse Picker-Outer— who unfortunately was growing very old and told The King he was going to retire. The King Horse Maven told this Super Talented Horse Picker-Outer he had to find his replacement before he left.

So this Super Talented Horse Picker-Outer interviewed far and wide, high and low, east and west, uptown and downtown—until he finally found someone he thought would make a fabulous Totally Wise Horse Picker-Outer Replacement. He shared the good news with the King Horse Maven—who requested this new replacement show a free sample of his speedy-horse picking skills!

This new Totally Wise Horse Picker-Outer Replacement was up for the challenge! He searched far and wide, high and low, east and west, uptown and downtown—until he found a truly speedy race horse! He announced the terrific good news to the King!

"What kind of horse is it?" The King Horse Maven asked.

"It's a beautiful golden-yellow stallion!" said the new Totally Wise Horse Picker-Outer Replacement.

"I can't wait to see it!" exclaimed The King Horse Maven. But when The King Horse Maven peeked into the field to see his new beautiful golden-yellow stallion, he saw instead a chocolate-brown colt! The King Horse Maven was furious—and immediately requested to see the old retiring Horse Picker-Outer, so he could yell at him!

"Your new replacement Horse-Picker-Outer is an idiot," The King began to yell. "Look in that field at the horse he found me! He described it as a golden yellow stallion—and it's a chocolate brown colt! Your replacement sucks big-time!"

But the old retiring Horse-Picker-Outer simply calmly smiled and said, "Actually this replacement is far more talented than I even thought! When he sees a horse he doesn't even notice if it's yellow or brown, or a stallion or a colt—all he sees is FAST HORSE RUNNING! The guy is brilliant!"

The King paused, reflected, smiled, agreed. "Ahhhhhh," said The King, "You've found me a brilliant Horse-Picker-Outer, indeed."

I LOVE THIS STORY! I want for you the same picker-outer skills for your Prince Charming! I want you to look at your Prince Crush—and not stay so focused on if he's blond or a brunette, tall or short—or any of those superficial lures. I want you to be able to focus mostly on what your Prince Crush is like *superinsidehimself!*

4. Does Your Man Have a Sweet Soul—Living Life in The Sweet Spot Of The Mean Zone?

I believe you need at least one **VERY** to fall in love. For example, it helps if your honey is **VERY** smart, or **VERY** talented, or **VERY** hardworking, or **VERY** full of interesting world lens comments, or **VERY** caring, or **VERY** funny or **VERY** supportive of you, etc.

Basically, you need to see at least one magical, heart-fluttering quality about this man that makes him stand out to you as special—for true love to spring forth. Does your partner have at least one **VERY** special thing that makes you all a-flutter? Simultaneously, although finding one **VERY** in your partner is **VERY** good, finding two **VERY** aspects can be **VERY** bad. For example, if your partner is **VERY**, **VERY** funny or even **VERY, VERY** hardworking or even **VERY VERY** into you—this person might be trouble— might be super-annoying due to this extra dosage of that quality—which takes him outside the "**MEAN ZONE**" moderation point for that quality—and far into an "**EXTREME ZONE**." Does your partner have any doubly **VERY** aspects that you see as being a potential "**EXTREME ZONE**" relationship-zapper? If so, talk with your partner about this as a **GROWTH OPPORTUNITY ZONE!**

5. Still Having Trouble Hearing The Difference Between Wedding Bells And Warning Bells?

If you want some help figuring out if you should break up or make up, I suggest you play a little **LOVE BINGO**. Coming up on the next 2 pages, I will be giving you two Bingo Boards. One has **WEDDING BELLS,** the other has **WARNING BELLS.**

Get a pen and cross off the squares that apply to your Prince Crush. When you're done, you will see which bingo board your Prince Crush offers you more of, **WEDDING BELLS** or **WARNING BELLS**. If you have more **WEDDING BELLS**, then I suggest you stay the path, and keep exploring if happily ever after love is awaiting you. If **WARNING BELLS** are aplenty, I suggest you might want to dump the chump.

If you're still confused about your Prince's nobility, meet me in Chapter 10, and I will explain a little something to you called **"LOVE MAXIMIZATION."**

LOVE BINGO:
Wedding Bells

Your man doubles your good times and halves your bad times?	You 2 have bad math, where $1 + 1 = 3$	Your man makes you more relaxed, inspired, more content.
If your man lost all his money or hair, you'd still love him.	Leaves cute e-mails/ messages	Generous in spoiling you
Generous in the bedroom	Has healthy relationship with parents	Introduces you to parents
Openly discusses thoughts on marriage	Listens with 20/20 hearing	Deals with conflict without breaking dishes or heart
Says that tongue twister, "You are right."	You both feel instinctive mutual trust.	You feel like your favorite, happiest, best self around him!

LOVE BINGO:
Warning Bells

Tsk, tsk . . . caught him in a lie	Tsk, tsk . . . caught him in a promise broken	Tsk, tsk . . . caught him in an act of total selfishness
Tsk, tsk...caught him in a compromising position	Calls his parents "mommy" or "daddy"	Calls his parents "@#!%&"
Treats strangers/ waiters/taxi drivers/ etc. rudely	Treats strangers waiters/taxi drivers/ etc. better than you	Flirts with your friends/parents/ sibling
Never available on weekends	Stonewalls when angry	He's always angry— rarely happy!
He doesnt want to talk about commitment.	He's full of inconsistencies that make him appear untrustworthy.	His friends have low character! They're bad apples falling near his tree!

CHAPTER

10

Warning: Don't Be A Love Maximizer

(Or You'll Minimize Your Chances For True Love!)

efore you even think about breaking up with your Prince Crush, I want to ask you a highly personal and important question:

Are you a gal who's known for never being satisfied—always complaining about what you have—and looking around for something better?

If so, your perfectionistic search for *"the better"* might be making your love life worse!

And that's not just my opinion—that's the opinion of Barry Schwartz, Ph.D.— the wonderful author of *The Paradox of Choice: Why More Is Less*—who has concluded that America's present *"excess proliferation of choice"* is making people more anxious and less happy—even clinically depressed! Schwartz describes folks who drive themselves nuts (and depressed) checking out every single option as "**MAXIMIZERS**."

ARE YOU A MAXIMIZER?

Do you always drive yourself nuts and depressed—questioning whether you're making the right choices—lovewise and otherwise—then later regret your choices lovewise and otherwise?

Unfortunately, in today's online world, it's very easy to become a "**LOVE MAXIMIZER**" with the tempting smorgasbord of dating choices constantly available. With so much choice, it's easy to fall into the temptation of seeking an "**UPGRADE IN LOVE**"— even when your sweetie is a total sweetie! Or you can wind up stuck in "**CHOICE PARALYSIS**"—never being able to fully commit to a relationship!

HOW DOES THIS HAPPEN?

Schwartz cites a study with shoppers. Group #1 was offered free samples of six different jams. Group #2 was offered free samples of 24 jams. Afterwards, Group #1 was more likely to buy a jam than Group #2. This result doesn't seem logical. You'd guess that people would be more likely to find a jam when given a range four times as large. But the over-abundance of choice seemed to freeze shoppers' decision-making skills.

Unfortunately, this same **CHOICE PARALYSIS** affect can happen to daters when shopping for partners in that endless online parade of possibilities. *"It's a satisfaction treadmill,"* says Schwartz. *"The more options we have available, the more we think that another option out there is perfect."*

THE TRUTH ACCORDING TO ME?

Rarely is anyone or anything perfect. And so the #1 biggest problem with choice: It's an illusion! Up-close and personal, all of that choice is not always grade-A material!

I also found another interesting—and scary—study that described how people who are exposed to a few minutes' worth of advertising (with its yummy assorted bon bon selection of nubile women and improbably handsome men) were more likely to experience greater discontent with their partner after viewing. Egads!

TRANSLATION: Love is not only suspect for being blind—it's suspect for being *blindsided!* A good relationship can be totally destroyed by the blazing promise of better options—which never really existed in the first place!

Tempted To Throw
Over Your Budding Love,
Because You Think The
Grass Is Budding Greener
On The Other Side? If so . . .

I. Recognize that being a "LOVE MAXIMIZER" actually minimizes your chances for finding happily ever after love! Realize that you luckily have a choice in how you view choice—and you can choose to see the problems in constantly going for illusory lures!

II. If right now you're tempted to two-time, think twice! (1) Remind yourself how all those other Prince Crushes who look so good from faraway will look not so good close up—when you can more clearly see their many Prince Harming flaws beneath their superficial yummy surface. (2) Remind yourself that you are a Princess Charming—a gal who puts in the virtue of **DISCIPLINE** and behaves with high integrity!

III. Accept right now that no one guy is ever going to have every single friggin' thing you need. The goal is to find a guy who embraces those 5 essential traits—and makes you feel like you're a Princess Charming prize—makes you feel loved, understood, safe, happy and inspired to grow into your best self!

IV. Every day, end your day by sharing out loud with your Prince Crush all the many qualities you love about him! Appreciation is a tremendous aphrodisiac—for both the giver and receiver! In fact, consistently shared appreciation will help ensure both you and your Prince Crush remain **LOVE ENERGIZERS**—instead of **LOVE MAXIMIZERS!**

Is Your Prince Crush A Prince Harming … ?

(View Breakups as A "Love Fullures," Not Failures!)

re you right now feeling as if your Prince Crush is turning out to be a Prince Harming—and so you're a Princess Friggin' Idiot? If so, stop beating yourself up—and instead start patting yourself on the back! You're learning important lessons about love, which will now bring you even closer to snagging that elusive and seemingly exclusive true love you are seeking! Albert Einstein said it well when he said:

"If I find 10,000 ways something won't work, I haven't failed. I am not discouraged, because every wrong attempt discarded is another step forward."

TRANSLATION: You gotta kiss a lot of frogs before you meet your Prince. Plus, you probably will have to kiss some pigs, dogs and jackasses. In fact, the frogs will be the easiest to kiss. The important thing is to rename all those amphibians (etc.) as your "Teachers." You must view all love "failures" as "fullures"—chock full of important love lessons to be learned!

Basically, you can never fail in life or love. You just produce results. It's up to you how you interpret those results.

There are no failed relationships. Every person in our lives has a life lesson to teach.

In this chapter I want to make sure you're on your way to learning the right life lessons—the lessons that will more swiftly lead you to **LIFE PLAN RIGHT**. I don't want you to learn what Aristotle called an **INCORRECT SYLLOGISM**. Back in the 300s BC, Aristotle coined the word "**SYLLOGISM**" to describe a verbal system for finding new universal truths. For example, one of his more famous **SYLLOGISMS** is:

All animals are mortal.
A man is an animal.
Therefore, a man is mortal.

After a bad breakup, I intuit you might be tempted to create the following **INCORRECT SYLLOGISM**:

Your ex is a jerk.
All men are like your ex.
Therefore, all men are jerks.

This above **SYLLOGISM** is just a plain ol' **"SILLY-OLOGISM"**—because it's breaking an important **SYLLOGISM** rule. You're not allowed to include an untruth in its formula! And you are wrong if you believe all men are like your ex! There are indeed many men out there who will lead you down the right path towards **LIFE PLAN RIGHT**! You just have to put in the virtue of **DISCIPLINE** to tap into your **CONSCIOUS INSIGHT** so as to make sure you're heading in the right direction!

Unfortunately, it's often difficult to see clearly when you're caught up in the midst of an emotional storm—like a breakup with a Prince Harming! Hence, it's important at breakup time to stop, relax, breathe, meditate and let the fog clear—so you can more assuredly see your life lessons—before you begin to move forwards—or you could wind up harming your sweet soul even more—by introducing your soul to yet another damaging Prince Harming!

In a way your soul is your vehicle for life. You need your soul to get you through the all of life. And so you must make sure your soul doesn't get damaged too much during stormy times! In particular, you must make sure your soul's rear view mirror doesn't get twisted after a stormy time—so you confuse it for your window on life—and remain looking backwards on all your mistakes.

LISTEN UP!

If your rear-view mirror gets twisted during a stormy time, and all you're staring at is your unforgiven, unlearned-from past, you might mistakenly find yourself driving back towards this same **LIFE PLAN WRONG** direction. Hence why I recommend that after a stormy emotional time, you stop and put in the effort to find a **BETTER LIFE MAP**—one which absolutely aims you in the direction of **LIFE PLAN RIGHT**.

Capiche? If not—or even if so—here is a Capiche-Enhancing poetic essay I've always loved.

Autobiography In Five Short Chapters
by Portia Nelson

Chapter I
I walk down the street.
There is a deep hole in
the sidewalk.
I fall in.
I am lost ... I am
helpless.
It isn't my fault.
It takes me forever to
find a way out.

Chapter II
I walk down the same
street.
There is a deep hole in
the sidewalk.
I pretend I don't see it.
I fall in again.
I can't believe I am in
the same place
but, it isn't my fault.
It still takes a long time
to get out.

Chapter III
I walk down the same
street.
There is a deep hole in
the sidewalk.
I see it is there.
I still fall in ... it's a
habit.
My eyes are open
I know where I am.
It is my fault.
I get out immediately.

Chapter IV
I walk down the same
street.
There is a deep hole in
the sidewalk.
I walk around it.

Chapter V
I walk down another
street.

It's funny. When I first read Portia Nelson's essay I thought it should end at Chapter IV—where I learn I am supposed to walk around the hole.

MEANING? I thought it was okay to simply stay dating Prince Harmings—as long as I figured out how to better troubleshoot with them.

But of course—duh—it makes far greater sense to just stop dating Prince Harmings altogether—and start heading down Prince Charming Road—the true happy lover's lane!

Ironically, life's worst of times (aka: breakups) are eventually what lead us to find our best of times— because they prompt us to **WAKE UP FROM OUR AUTO-PILOT SLUMBERS**—tap into our human perk of **CONSCIOUS INSIGHT**—so we can finally get ourselves out of those damn potholes and aimed towards **LIFE PLAN RIGHT!**

I believe that much of what makes us angry about the challenges in life is having a **LIFE PLAN A** we fall in love with—which then does not work out—and so we're pissed off that we have to pursue a **LIFE PLAN B**.

If you want to tame your inner demons, you must consciously choose to never become too obsessively attached to a particular **LIFE PLAN A**. Embracing detachment as a way of life will always give you a healthier sense of peacefulness when you land plunked into life's potholes!

*In a way, the definition for enlightenment is: The quiet acceptance of what is—and an open mind to embrace **LIFE PLAN B**!*

I personally have found that I can more readily accept not getting a **LIFE PLAN A**, when I get myself excited about a new **LIFE PLAN B**! I also remind myself how often enough my **LIFE PLAN B** turns out to be something far better than my original **LIFE PLAN A** was ever going to be!

FOR EXAMPLE

By ending my relationship with my last Prince Harming (my supposed **LIFE PLAN A**—and definite "Teacher") I was then led into the arms of my now Prince Charming—who is in truth a far happier **LIFE PLAN A.**

*Interestingly enough, early on in Aristotle's life, he was forced to deal with giving up a **LIFE PLAN A** and surrender instead to a **LIFE PLAN B**!*

Originally, Aristotle had planned to become a physician like his dear ol' dad—the King of Macedonia's private doctor, no less! Then Aristotle's dad suddenly died, and instead of going pre-med, Aristotle was forced to go to Athens to study in Plato's Academy, where he soon became the Michael Jordan of philosophy.

I love this little resumé tidbit on Aristotle— because it proves Aristotle practiced what he preached about appropriately dealing with stormy times. Aristotle didn't let his father's sudden passing blow him sideways or Bonsai him downwards. After this tragedy, Aristotle consciously swayed with the winds of chance and challenge, ultimately allowing these winds to blossom him into his **MIGHTIEST HUMAN BEING SELF**—and lead him to tap into his **UNIQUE SPECIFIC FUNCTION** as a brilliant philosopher.

*Aristotle's **LIFE PLAN B** of becoming a philosopher definitely seems to be his true **LIFE PLAN A**.*

Similarly, right now you might be hurt over how your Prince Harming did not turn out to be your **LIFE PLAN A** love adventure. But you must stay peaceful inside, knowing that your **LIFE PLAN B** Prince Charming will turn out to be twice the **LIFE PLAN A** man your friggin' ex-Prince Harming guy could ever have been to you!

I want to make sure a new improved love story unfolds for you! Below, I want you to write all the love lessons your ex-Prince Harming taught you!

WHY MY EX-PRINCE HARMING IS MY TEACHER:

I. Thanks to my Teacher, I learned in my next relationship I need to find a man who offers: _____

_____

_____

_____.

II. Thanks to my Teacher, I learned in my next relationship I need to feel more: _____

_____
_____.

III. Thanks to my Teacher, I learned in my next
relationship I need to feel less: _____

_____
_____.

IV. Thanks to my Teacher, I learned in my next
relationship I insist my man bring with him the
following deal makers: _____

_____
_____.

Still feeling miffed that your ex-Prince Harming
Teacher did not turn out to be your **LIFE PLAN A
LOVE STORY?** Shut up, cheer up—and fill yourself up
with the following positive thoughts!

How To Keep Your Love Fullure Lessons Full:

I. It's normal for you to feel hurt right now at breakup time! But you should feel proud of yourself too—
for risking at almighty love—and getting to feel so
many passionate feelings. Aristotle said:

*"We live in deeds, not years; in thoughts not breaths; in
feelings, not in figures on a dial. We should count time
by heart throbs. He most lives who thinks most, feels
the noblest, acts the best."*

TRANSLATION: I think what Aristotle was saying is that life has ebbs and flows. There's no such thing as endless flow. Unfortunately life can sometimes feel like ebb, ebb, ebb, brief-flash-of-flow, more ebb, ebb, ebb. But every ebb always offers the opportunity to think a new thought flavor and feel a new emotion flavor. The more varied the flavors of life you get to taste, the more interesting, layered, educated, self-developed, world-experienced and mightier You will be!

II. Remind yourself how it's always your choice. You can be miserable. Or you can motivate yourself to stretch your mind—and seek out better interpretations for your break up! Remind yourself to choose the positive belief that you've learned the necessary lessons that transform your **LIFE PLAN B LOVE STORY** into something far better than your original **LIFE PLAN A!**

III. Remind yourself how it's normal for the average person to weakly give in and give up when love disappoints! But you're far from average! You're a Princess Charming. You're the type of girl who puts in the **VIRTUES OF COURAGE AND DISCIPLINE** not to be weak—and instead stay aimed at your final purpose: soul-nurturing love happiness! You're the type of girl who makes the world say YES to you!

IV. Whenever you're tempted to think negative thoughts about your Prince Harming Teacher, ask yourself: "Are these thoughts leading me forwards to **LIFE PLAN RIGHT**—or backwards to **LIFE PLAN WRONG?**" Put in the **VIRTUE OF DISCIPLINE** to only choose thoughts which move you *forwards*! Use this word *"forwards"* as your mantra every time a negative belief enters your head!

V. Recognize that bumper sticker you've read on cars is oh so true:

"It is better to have loved and lost ... than to live with a wacko for the rest of your life."

Finally ... let me end this chapter with some helpful thoughts that ensure your **LOVE FULLURE** stays full!

If you're eager to get married swiftly—guess what? Many psychologists, sociologists, married folks, and divorced folks all agree:

When it comes to marriage, it's better late than early!

Studies consistently show that many folks who marry younger in life do so for the wrong reasons or without the right perspectives on what empowers a union to work. Similarly, more of the folks who marry later do so for wiser reasons and with a more well-thought-out perspective.

WHY IT'S WISER TO WAIT TO WED:

I. You've had the breakups that led to breakdowns that led to the breakthrough.

II. You've sowed your wild oats—and now think, "Sow what?" All those tempting choices aren't really so tempting—they're merely **RELATIONSHIPS OF PLEASURE** or **RELATIONSHIPS OF UTILITY.**

III. You're healthier and more together—meaning the relationship now has at least a 50 percent chance of being healthier and staying together—because you're doing the work to become your **MIGHTIEST HUMAN BEING SELF.**

IV. You now wisely know the "ability to compromise" is very, very sexy.

V. You no longer confuse "conflict" for "passion." Rather than choosing a partner who keeps you walking on eggshells—it's essential you choose someone as comforting as listening to seashells—a partner who keeps you at your most safe and secure—that's what a **RELATIONSHIP OF SHARED VIRTUE** is all about!

VI. You've wisely stopped looking for *"sex objects"*— and have started looking for *"long-term relationship objects."* **MEANING?** You are less likely to marry due to a sizzling lust which can become fizzling lust very quickly. Basically, you now wisely know seeking *"long-haul qualities"* are what make for a Prince Charming—and *"short-haul qualities"* are what make for a Prince Harming!

VII. You now know that just because a person looks good on papyrus doesn't mean they're going to "act good" in real life. Status, wealth, fame and trust funds no longer blindly seduce you towards a Prince Harming!

VIII. You now know not to become intimately involved with someone who has the following: **RED FLASHING WARNING LIGHTS BLINKING BLINDINGLY IN YOUR FACE!**

IX. You're now wisely less "self-centered" about problem-solving—and more "relationship-centered." **MEANING?** You recognize it's better to be wrong some of the time—and do the work that leads to growth, which leads to a happily ever after love future.

X. You now know it's never a checklist of adjectives to look for in a person—but the compatibility of your adjectives with their adjectives. **MEANING?** The rocks in your head must fit in the holes in the other person's head. You each need to value dealing with conflict in a loving and empathic way

XI. You now know personality is the tip of the iceberg. But character is the real foundation. While it's okay not to share all the same interests and hobbies, you must always share the same core character values and ethics!

XII. You now wisely know you're never going to find perfect, custom-fit love in a world of off-the-rack people. All people will have some flaws and misfittings.

XIII. It's now apparent what was inappropriate behavior in your parents! **MEANING?** You are now more aware of how not to share your parents' "Inappropriate Behavior Issues" with your partner!

XIV. After having endured a gazillion awful dates, suddenly your fear of working at a relationship is a lot less scary than your fear of more awful dates.

XV. You now know when a relationship is on the road to nowhere—and how to find that exit ramp away from Emotionally Unavailable Territory.

XVI. You're less needy and more want-y. Meaning? You don't "need" a mate in your life. You want one. And so you are less likely to be unhealthfully co-dependent—and more likely to be healthfully inter-dependent.

XVII. You now have work you love—so can put more attention on the work of love.

XVIII. Together you both are making more money than ever—perhaps doubling your combined income—which can mean halving some of the monetary stress.

XIX. Instead of being reactive—you're now proactive. You wait for the smoke to clear from the explosive glitches you have in your "Relationship Disagreement Areas." Indeed, you are constantly looking for ways to permanently remove repeated glitches from the system of your "Relationship Disagreement Areas"—so explosions don't keep on happening.

XX. You now wisely know "communication" is about "listening"—just as much as it's about talking—and thereby you now listen with 20/20 hearing.

XXI. You now know having a firmer tush won't snag you a good mate—but having a strong gut and listening to it will!

XXII. You now see love as a two-way street—not a rollercoaster ride.

XXIII. You now know true love requires love of truth. You must share openly and vulnerably with your partner to feel true intimacy and avoid long-term problems. With this in mind, you now also know that if you seek a partner by using gameplaying bait, you will only lure in gameplaying fish. However if you use open/honest communication bait you will lure in open/honest communication fish—the best kind of relationship fish to marry!

XXIV. You now recognize that you get love in your life by loving your life. Meaning: A man or a woman isn't meant to be your entire life—they're meant to enhance the happy life you've created for yourself, which has many supportive people and inspiring interests.

XXV. You know size does matter. You need a partner with a really big heart. Nice guys and girls don't finish last—they create relationships that last!

XXVI. You've stopped blaming your past for bad relationships—and started blaming your present. **MEANING?** You are finally exploring what you're doing to bring a relationship down—taking self-responsibility. You've witnessed your "constants" in a variety of relationship settings—and thereby know when you're the trouble-maker.

XXVII. Having less time to waste in your life magically increases your intelligence and instincts with people.

XXVIII. You know who you are—so you have a higher percentage probability of finding someone who's right for you. After all, by now you've had years to research jobs to have, cities to live in, people to date. It's as if you hold a Ph.D. in knowing thyself.

XIX. You now wisely also know who you are not—so you have a higher percentage probability of finding someone who's NOT right for you.

XXX. You now wisely know love is a boomerang. What you have and give away is what you get back.

XXXI. Hey, we now live longer—so ironically even if you mary in your forties, you can still wind up being married for 50+ years—that is if you wait to marry for the right **RELATIONSHIP OF SHARED VIRTUE REASONS**—and are cutting back on the bacon cheeseburgers!

HOW YOU FEELING? Are you getting psyched about your **LIFE PLAN B LOVE STORY** becoming your true **LIFE PLAN A?** I want to drill this optimistic belief into your brain grooves—so your neurons are all abuzz with faith that your Prince Charming is on the way!

With this in mind, I want you to reread your *"living happily ever after with your Prince Charming visualization"* I had you write at the beginning of this book—and rewrite it! Include the lessons your Prince Harming Teacher taught you—so these lessons become clear priorities when you start doing your Prince Charming Shopping!

_____

_____

_____

_____

GUESS WHAT? I confidently know you're on your way to finding your Prince Charming! Because I am so certain, coming up in this final chapter I will be giving you lots of insights on how to make sure your love with your Prince Charming lasts till death do you part—instead of lasting until you both want to kill each other! Seriously, I recognize how I began this book by assigning you 30 days of looking at your **LOVE VISUALIZATIONS** and your **VISION BOARD**. But those 30 days were simply the teeny weeny beginning of a *"living happily ever after future!"* With this in mind, in this final chapter I am going to offer you some **LIFELONG PRINCE CHARMING LOVE BOOSTERS!** Meet you in Chapter 12!

CHAPTER

12

Is Your Prince Crush A Prince Charming...?

(Tips To Ensure You Stay On Your Path To
Living Happily Ever After)

So, it finally happened. You lucked out and met someone you feel could be "the" one—versus the usual just another one. You're excited. With this exuberance comes the urge to run not walk towards marriage. You tell yourself if you feel this strongly, it must be real—so why fake otherwise? You're not into playing games.

BUT THE TRUTH IS:

You could be playing a big game with yourself if you rush your crush into marriage. Your rushing might not be fueled by sheer almighty desire—but by an insecure need to control the relationship.

PLUS, HERE'S A BIG IRONY: Rushing love actually leads to less control—because often when you rush that crush you're more likely to crash that crush! Many people who move speedily towards marriage wind up scaring off their partner—or even unwittingly scaring off themselves.

PLUS, HERE'S A BIG IRONY, PART TWO: It doesn't matter how fast you get somewhere if you're heading in the wrong direction. Often, when you rush a crush, you don't gather enough important information that could better help you suss out if you're psyched about someone with long-term warm and loving compatibility **(RELATIONSHIP OF SHARED VIRTUE)**—or merely riled up over short-term hot lustful chemistry **(RELATIONSHIP OF PLEASURE AND/OR UTILITY).**

For all these reasons, often speed kills when it comes to love. *(Note: I also don't recommend speed for dieting. I once did it—and all it made me do was eat faster.)*

Just think about what happens when you move slowly versus quickly down a street in a car. If you drive slowly—you notice many more details. If you speed, you just get a big blur of data. Well, this goes ditto on dating data. If you head towards marriage slowly, you're more likely to notice those deal breakers and problematic issues staring you in the face. Conversely, if you rush on in towards marriage, you might not be able to handle those dangerous personality curves and surprise emotional potholes.

Yes, it's rather ironic that this need for speed comes from hoping to gain more certainty about the future, and instead leads to a lot less control—well, as if any control at all is ever possible!

WHICH BRINGS ME TO A BIG IRONY, PART THREE: Control and certainty do not exist. Even quantum physicists can't control the movement of a particle in a petrie dish. And if a super smart physicist can't control one of the teeniest objects on this planet, well, you're no better off trying to control your relationship.

I know from whence I speaketh. On two different occasions I have had two different men ask me to marry them—after merely knowing me for a little over a month. Onward we began racing to the altar—while my heart raced a bit too quickly—and soon my feelings were altered.

I began having what I called "**STRANGE FREUDIAN MISREADS.**" At one point I misread a sign in a store window, thinking it read **"MARITAL AIDS"**—when it really read **"MARTIAL ARTS."** Another time I misread an article in a magazine talking about **"LOVE MATES"** as the scary words: **"LOVE MATS."** I misread an e-mail talking about **"TYING THAT KNOT"**—as a desire for slipping a noose around my neck.

Obviously I was feeling scared about moving at this speed of flight! Unfortunately, whenever I tried to slow things down, each of these men pushed even harder for marriage—acted out with anger and overly-controlling behavior—which simply pushed me further away—because I did not feel safe, heard, understood, nurtured.

As these relationships progressed, I gathered some important dating data that was evidence that these men had some Prince Harming negative qualities—and were each lacking in important character virtues for a happily ever after future. They thereby each became my Teachers about what I needed to prioritize looking for moving forward—and teach me they did.

That was then, this is now.

Today I am with a fabulous Prince Charming who makes me feel safe, heard, understood, nurtured. When I told my present Prince Charming how I need to move forward at a comfortable pace, he heard me clearly—and continues to want to hear me clearly. He's always checking in with me about how I am feeling about our relationship, our communication, our sex life, our mutual goals, our mutual feelings.

THE LESSON LEARNED?

When you're with the right man, you won't need to speed-race to the altar. You will know this man will be in your life forever, so there's no need to rush. Forever is a long time to be with someone—so what's the hurry?

When you're with the right man, neither of you will be able to envision a future without one another, so you will feel safe and comfortable to always speak your truth—and know you will feel safe, heard, understood, nurtured—and vice versa for your partner.

Indeed, I feel very safe, heard, understood, and nurtured by my Prince Charming—who is always saying the sweetest things about my being *"the woman of his dreams"* and *"wanting me to be with him to his final days."*

Not only do I feel safe, loved, understood and nurtured, I feel appreciative of him, dammit. And I share my appreciation with him out loud as often as possible.

After snagging my Prince Charming, I also feel a strong belief in the miracle powers of visualization—because everything I wrote about wanting to snag in a *"living happily ever after in love"* future is now a reality. Here's a peek at some of what I wrote in my visualization:

"I am happily dating a man who is wanting me to be exclusive with him—and I want to be exclusive with him! This man feels that by meeting me and spending time with me his life is better than ever—and I feel the same. I make him feel more JOYFUL, more STABLE, more INSPIRED, more SUPPORTED, and SAFE to become his fullest self —and he makes me feel more JOYFUL, more STABLE, more INSPIRED, more SUPPORTED and SAFE to become my fullest self. My loving partner values growth and good communication—he is monogomous, trustworthy, a good communicator, a good listener, loving, lovable, sexy, sensual, smart, funny, adventurous, fun—and feels as if I am a PRIZE! I am the same virtues and qualities with him—and feel he is a PRIZE as well. He loves to share his life with me, share his friends with me, share his family with me—and I am happy to share it all with him as well."

GUESS WHAT?

I wrote this visualization down over a year ago—and consciously chose to read it every day three times a day—until now I live it every day—24 hours a day!

GUESS WHAT ELSE?

I still keep rereading my visualization—even though I've now found my Prince Charming—so as to remind myself to stay on path to living this highly loving form of love—to prompt me not to allow our love to unconsciously, lazily spiral downward. In fact, whenever I feel myself tempted to not tap into *those* **VIRTUES OF COURAGE AND DISCIPLINE** when dealing with a Prince Charming problem, I reread my visualization. I'm then once again reminded of how much I longed for finding a man with the qualities my man offers. Soon enough, I'm highly motivated to tap into those **VIRTUES OF COURAGE** and **DISCIPLINE** and speak up warmly about whatever is weighing heavily on my mind and heart.

Back in the beginning of this book I shared this favorite Aristotle quote:

"Wishing to be in love is quick work, but love is a slow, ripening fruit."

After you've found your almighty Prince Charming love, it's important you keep putting in the **VIRTUES OF COURAGE AND DISCIPLINE** to make sure your love remains fresh, ripening and always growing. Unfortunately, often we humans forget to appreciate the love we've found after we've found it—and thereby put our love at risk of getting bruised or going bad.

HERE'S THE DEAL ON LOVE:

If you're saying *"I love you!"* out loud to someone, you must make sure your actions remain in sync with your words! If you start to feel you can coast on simply saying *"I love you!"* out loud, without showing love, eventually you will chew all of the flavor out of these words!

IN SUMMARY

It's far more important to show your love than to say your love!

How To Show And Tell Your Love So It Stays Ripening And Growing:

I. Regularly check in with your Prince Charming about how he feels about his life goals and dreams. Encourage him to talk about his **UNIQUE SPECIFIC FUNCTION.** Men feel happiest when they're successfully enjoying their **UNIQUE SPECIFIC FUNCTION.** Ask your Prince Charming how you can help to honor his dreams!

II. If you're living together or spending long stretches of time together, always be sure to pepper up your schedule with spicy romantic dates out on the town. Revisit the places where you originally fell for one another—to get **TRIGGER HAPPY**!

III. Make sure you're enjoying a **HOT SENSUAL LIFE** along with your **HOT SEXUAL LIFE.** For example, hold his hand while walking down the street—or even while watching TV.

IV. Send him sexy and/or sweet and/or motivational texts during the day—so he feels safe, supported and nurtured.

V. Chris Rock offered up the following funny quip: "What do men want? I'll tell you what men want! Food, sex and silence!" Although this was meant as a joke, there's a smidge of truth within it! Sometimes men feel we women stereotypically tell stories which go on far too loooooong. Become aware of keeping your stories short and sweet. In fact regularly and consciously give your man the gift of less gab. For an entire evening, listen 80%, talk 20%.

VI. Psychologists say the best time to talk about your relationship problems is when you're not having any —so tempers remain calm. On a happy evening out, ask your partner how you could do even better at making him happier in the relationship! I think far too many people think after they have found a great love—that's it—they found it, so that's it, kaput! They can sit back and enjoy—not putting in any work. However that's like going on a job search— finding a great job—then thinking you can just sit at your desk—not doing any work. If you want to live happily ever after, you must put in the **VIRTUE OF DISCIPLINE** to work at your relationship ever after.

VII. When I wrote my bestffselling book *HOW TO MAKE YOUR MAN BEHAVE IN 21 DAYS OR LESS USING THE SECRETS OF PROFESSIONAL DOG TRAINERS* I meant it to be merely a humorous book to make girls laugh about love. But it did include some seriously helpful love advice—about a little something called **FLIGHT AND CHASE BEHAVIOR.** If you find your man is pulling back from you at times, keep in mind this dog trainer wisdom. Dog trainers say if your dog is running away from you, the worst thing in the world is to run after it. The dog will only run away faster. Instead you must remain calm. The animal can sense the fear and anxiety in you. Act like you're having lots of fun. The animal just wants be where the fun is. Being happy and having fun is highly attractive energy to be around!

VIII. Hopefully by now you are a complete believer in Aristotle's literally "life-changing philosophy" that happiness is about growing into your highest potential. With this in mind, consider yourself an ongoing student, eager to gather lots of new **CONSCIOUS INSIGHTS**. When at parties or group dinners, start up conversations about love with individuals who have happy relationships. Ask them why they think their relationships are thriving. What bumps did they endure? How did they manage to ride out their bumps? Why did they decide to ride out their bumps? Why do they think they're still enjoying their love ride? Share the principles from this book with them—and enjoy lively dialogues which might bring you and others new **CONSCIOUS INSIGHTS.**

IX. Consistently keep planning things to look forward to together as a couple in the next 3 weeks, 2 months, 1 year, 2 years, 5 years, etc.—so you two can keep your eyes on the prize of *living a happily ever after love future together!*

X. Whenever you feel your love is ebbing or your rage is flowing, take a good long look at your **VISION BOARD** and your **LOVE VISUALIZATION**—so you stay reminded about how much you value being with your Prince Charming. Remember: Whenever you can increase your **WHYPOWER**, you will increase your **WILLPOWER**. Staring at your **VISION BOARD** and your **LOVE VISUALIZATION** will help you to tap into those **VIRTUES OF COURAGE AND DISCIPLINE** so you remain operating at your *Mightiest Princess Charming Self* level!

XI. Visit me at my Web site *www.notsalmon.com* to get more love tips through my free Be Happy Dammit free newsletter! And write to me at *Karen@ notsalmon.com* to share with me your Living Happily Ever After Love Story! I want to hear all the happily ever after love details—so I can share how you turned your **"TALE OF WOE"** into a **"TALE OF WOW"** with others—and motivate as many women as possible to believe that true happily ever after love is indeed out there for them! You can also find me on **FACEBOOK** under my name "Karen Salmansohn" and on **TWITTER** at "notsalmon." I'm always posting empowering love tips to inspire and motivate folks to live their happiest ever after lives!

TO SUM IT UP—YOU GOTTA REMEMBER: IT'S CALLED A LOVE LIFE—NOT AN ANGST LIFE—NOR A I WANT TO STRANGLE HIM LIFE!

TO SUM IT UP—YOU GOTTA REMEMBER: YOUR FINAL ENDS IN LIFE SHOULD ALWAYS BE TO LIVE HAPPILY EVER AFTER—NEVER TO BE CONFUSED WITH LIVING PLEASURABLY EVER AFTER!

Or as my buddy (and now your buddy) Aristotle once said :

"Happiness is the meaning and the purpose of life, the whole aim and end of human existence, dammit!"

Okay. I admit it. I added the *dammit* onto that quote. But I'm intuiting if Aristotle were here now, he'd want to add on that *dammit* for emphasis to ensure you are indeed on your way to living and loving happily ever after, dammit!